IN NO TIME

PC
Basics

IN NO TIME

PC
Basics

Oliver Pott

Edited by
ROB YOUNG

 Prentice Hall Europe

London New York Toronto Sydney Tokyo Singapore Madrid Mexico City Munich Paris

First published in 1997 as Easy – PC-Grundlagen by
Markt&Technik Buch- und Software Verlag GmbH
85540 Haar bei München/Germany

This edition published 1999 by
Prentice Hall Europe
Campus 400, Maylands Avenue
Hemel Hempstead
Hertfordshire, HP2 7EZ

A division of
Simon & Schuster International Group

Translated by Ian Gronbach and Janet Richmond
in association with First Edition Translations Limited, Cambridge

Typeset in Stone Sans
by Malcolm Smythe and Michael Weintroub

Designed and Produced by Bender Richardson White

Printed and bound in Great Britain
by TJ International Ltd, Padstow Cornwall

Library of Congress Cataloging-in-Publication Data
Available from the publisher
British Library Cataloguing in Publication Data
A catalogue record for this book is available from the British Library

ISBN 0-13-977638-9

1	2	3	4	5	02	01	00	99	98

4

Contents

4 From man to the computer — 60

5 Digital documents — 92

6 How your computer works — 146

Paper and computers ——— 168

Almost like television ——— 194

Internet and on-line ——— 208

7

10 The 'personal computer' — 230

11 Software — 244

Useful information — 254

Glossary — 266

Index of key words — 320

Dear readers,

It is obvious that there are many advantages to working on a PC. After all, millions of professional users world-wide cannot be wrong, and we can no longer imagine offices without the electronic computing brains.

Perhaps you are one of those PC owners who want to use computers out of personal interest and have now treated yourself to a brand new machine. Or your job requires you to work with the technology, for example, because your accounts are computerised.

If this is the first contact you have had with the 'super typewriter', which is what a computer appears to be, then you have got hold of the right book. Perhaps you already work on a PC and now want to get to know your electronic colleague better. This book is also suitable for that as it introduces you to the PC basics in a structured way.

Emphasis is placed on practical knowledge and its direct application. Clear steps give you the information you need for your everyday work. If you want to use this book at the computer you can follow what is being shown 'live' as it were.

Have fun reading this book

On the next three pages you will see how your computer keyboard is laid out. To make it clearer for you, only certain blocks of keys are shown at once. Many of the computer keys have the same function as on a typewriter. There are, however, some additional keys that are geared to the peculiarities of computer work.

See for yourself . . .

Typewriter keys

You use these keys exactly as you do on a typewriter.
You also use the Enter key to send commands to the computer.

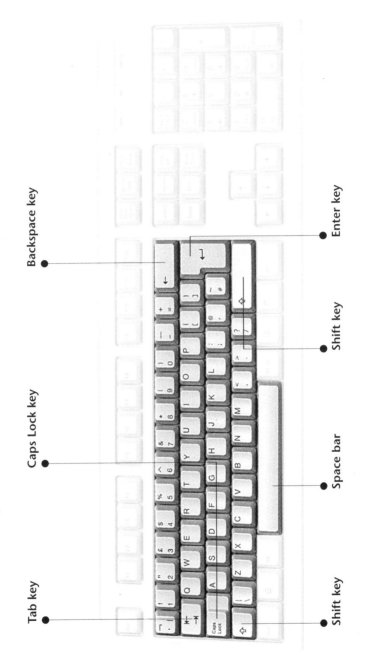

Backspace key

Caps Lock key

Tab key

Enter key

Shift key

Space bar

Shift key

11

Special keys, function keys, numeric keypad, status lights

When operating the computer, special keys and function keys, Ctrl, Alt and Alt Gr, are used for particular tasks, usually in combination with other keys. You can interrupt commands with the Escape key and insert or delete text with Insert and Delete.

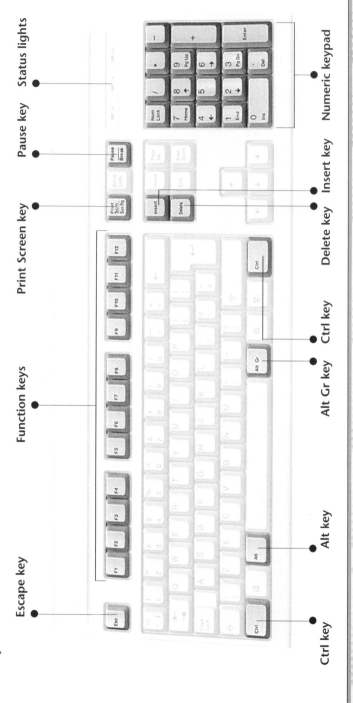

Escape key

Function keys

Print Screen key

Pause key

Status lights

Numeric keypad

Insert key

Delete key

Ctrl key

Alt Gr key

Alt key

Ctrl key

Navigational keys

You move about the screen with these keys.

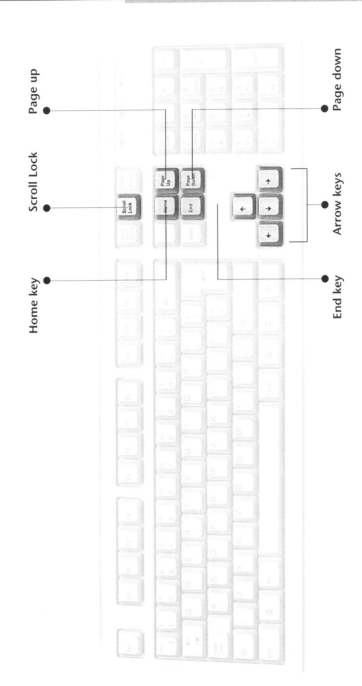

Page up

Scroll Lock

Home key

Page down

Arrow keys

End key

'Click . . . '
means: briefly press
a button once.

Click with the
left mouse
button . . .

Click with the
right mouse
button . . .

'Double-click . . . '
means: press the left
button twice in quick
succession.

Double-click

'Drag . . . '
means: click on certain screen items
with the left mouse button, hold
the button down, move the
mouse and so drag the item
to another position.

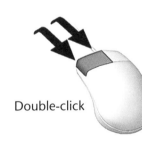

Drag

1

Unpacking, Setting-up and Getting to grips

What's in this chapter?

Before we introduce you to the diverse world of the computer we'll help you unpack and set up your PC. Starting the new PC for the first time is a particularly exciting moment.

You can miss out this chapter if your PC is already running or if you want to use the subject-matter as a 'dry run', as it were.

Your are going to learn:

17

1st Step: Peace and Time

If you have collected your PC from a PC dealer or department store and want to assemble it in your office or on the desk at home you need in particular some:

peace and time!

The technical term for connecting the individual pieces of equipment is installation

A PC cannot simply be plugged into the socket and switched on. It is not a good idea just to brak off what you're doing and think you can quickly return to it, particularly if you have never worked with a PC before.

Give yourself an hour or two to get used to the basics of the 'unfamiliar computer thing'. All the individual parts must be correctly connected for the PC to operate properly.

2nd Step: Unpacking and Setting up

Hardware is the technical term for the individual parts that fit together to make the computer. The complete PC is also described as the computer system or system for short

You will probably be wondering why the computer dealer gave you several boxes. Each box contains a component of the hardware you have bought.

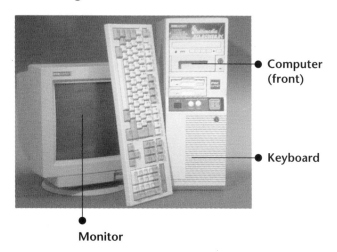

- Computer (front)
- Keyboard

Monitor

Check that you have the following boxes and then unpack the individual parts.

A tip for unpacking the individual parts: the computer monitor and the actual PC are packed in styrofoam for protection. This packaging often jams in the box.

Lie the box on its side and carefully remove the box from the styrofoam, rather than lifting the heavy monitor out of the box!

Now you can remove the styrofoam from the hardware and put it back in the box.

Computer box: This box contains the actual PC. You will recognise the PC by the numerous connectors at the back. This box often contains a number of user manuals, spare parts and perhaps a key in plastic bags. You will usually find the keyboard here as well, often in another small box;

Monitor box: The monitor is packed in another box. When you unpack it be careful that you do not damage the fragile screen;

Printer box: Your printer (if you have bought one) is packed in another box. In addition to the printer, the box contains a user manual and a toner cartridge or ribbon as well as several disks.

When you buy a printer always insist on having a printer cable. The printer is connected to the computer with this cable, which unfortunately is not supplied with your printer.

Now move the computer to where you want it. Put the monitor on your desk so that there is at least 50 cm between your eyes and the screen. Incidentally, the front of the computer is not the side with the numerous connectors. Tip: Often you will recognise the front by the manufacturer's square logo or other symbol.

Now put the keyboard, which is similar to a typewriter, on the work surface so that you are able to work at it comfortably.

19

The computer mouse should be to the right of your keyboard so that you can easily reach it when working. Ideally the mouse should sit on a mouse mat.

You can put the printer anywhere. However, a standard cable to connect it to the PC is a maximum of 2 metres long.

3rd Step: Connecting

When you were unpacking you will have noticed lots of cables that need to be connected with your PC. The individual pieces of equipment, for example the printer, exchange data with each other via these cables.

Incidentally: a 'pin' is a metal peg which
you will see if you look closely at a
connector. A '5 pin connector' is, therefore,
a connector with five metal pegs

Follow these instructions which will help you connect up the PC:

1 The mains cables . . .

. . . supply your PC,
monitor and printer with
power from the socket.
They each require a cable.
First put the correct end in
the back of your PC (you
cannot get this wrong;

Mains
outlet

only one connector fits!), monitor and printer. Then you can
connect the equipment to the mains; a three-way trailing socket
comes in useful here.

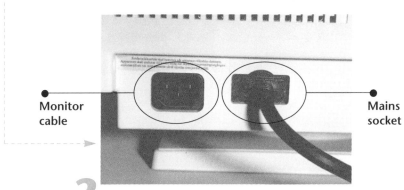

Monitor
cable

Mains
socket

2 The monitor cable . . .

. . . connects your PC with the monitor. It is
always built into the monitor and only fits in
one place at the back of the computer. Two
fixing screws prevent the connector from
slipping. Tighten these with a small screwdriver.

21

Printer cable

3 The printer cable . . .

. . . connects your printer to the PC. The wide
cable also only fits in one place and is secured
with two metal clips, or occasionally with
screws as well, to prevent it slipping.

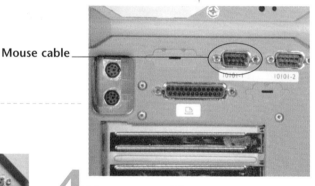

Mouse cable

Keyboard
cable

4 The mouse cable . . .

. . . also ends up at the back of
your PC. It is narrower than the
printer cable and has nine pins.

5 The keyboard cable . . .

. . . connects the keyboard. It is wound in a spiral and
ends in the keyboard. The other, round end fits in the
appropriate place at the back of your PC.

4th Step: The first time . . .

. . . you switch on is an exciting moment. When you press the 'on' button (it may be marked 'power') on the front of your computer a green light (the technical term is 'light-emitting diode') indicates that the PC is being supplied with power.

The start up procedure is also called powering up or booting.

Your monitor must be switched on separately. The 'on' switch for this is usually at the front, but on some models it is on the right-hand side or even at the back.

At this point do not press any keys on the keyboard. Instead watch the start up procedure of the PC. The screen, which is black at first, fills with strange characters and incomprehensible words.

After a minute or two, the black screen gives way to a colour (and much more reassuring!) display.

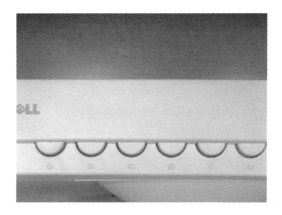

You can adjust the picture to suit you using the contrast and brightness controls on the monitor, as you can with your television.

Congratulations!

Your PC is now ready for you to have a go at working with it. In the following chapters we will guide you through it!

2

What's in this chapter?

You will see that humans and computers are related in certain ways.

You will learn how a computer processes information, what tasks modern computers can perform and what is left to humans to do.

You will learn how a computer records and reproduces a piece of music.

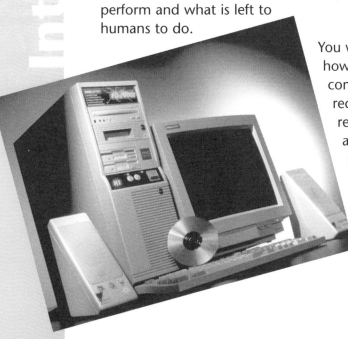

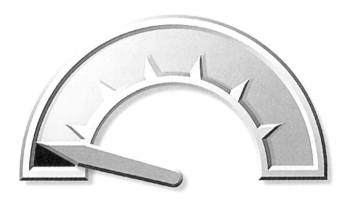

Your are going to learn about:

The history of computers – a young technology

The question that is perhaps most often asked by new computer users is 'What can a computer do?'

This cannot be answered in one sentence and even leaves PC experts struggling for words. Modern computer technology has become so extensive that it is often difficult to give a general answer.

Let's take a look back at the origins of modern computer technology, and then consider the question about the areas it can be used in.

In 1936 – more than 60 years ago – Konrad Zuse, who is considered to be the father of the computer, built the first compute, known as Zuse 1. In the absence of manufactured components, Zuse used telephone relays, connecting up 2000 of them to form a calculating machine. Zuse's computer was so large that it could have easily filled a whole house.

The first theoretical foundations of computer history had been laid. Compared with other technologies, at the age of 60 computer technology is still very young. The application range of the first computer was admittedly very limited; any modern solar-powered calculator costing just a few pounds, would have been far superior to the Zuse 1.

The ENIAC computer, which was developed in 1946 by the Americans Eckert and Mauchley, was much more powerful. Unlike the Zuse 1, the new development did not operate with telephone relays but used purely electronic components.

The ENIAC was certainly very powerful for its time, but had some disadvantages. The technology used was unwieldy, susceptible to interference and, to exaggerate, needed its own power station to operate.

Developments continued at a great pace, and in 1954 the history of computers underwent a full-blown renaissance. A new technology was introduced that year which is used in computers to this day: silicon chips. These tiny components had characteristics that made them ideal for use in electronic computers. About four years later, in 1958, Texas Instruments brought out an electronic computer chip which was the predecessor of the modern computer.

The personal computer, like the one you presumably have, only has to look back only 20 years to find its first direct forebears. In 1976 two American electronics students built the first 'personal computer'. Steven Jobs and Steve Wozniak called their new system Apple and set up a company with the same name which still exists today.

However, for some time to come, the newly created marvel remained in the shadow of other, more established technologies.

It was only when the market and industry leader IBM brought out its own personal computer in 1981 that the public began to show an interest in the new system.

The new computer was fitted with a computer chip (processor) made by Intel and was supplied with software by Microsoft, a hitherto unknown company. IBM/Intel/Microsoft: this triumvirate was the new star shining in the computer firmament, and even today terms such as 'IBM-compatible', 'Intel processor' or 'Microsoft Windows' are established parts of computer jargon.

While Intel and Microsoft still maintain their hold on the fiercely contested computer market, IBM lost its monopolistic position long ago. Today, due to the release of the underlying technical specifications, IBM-compatible computers can be manufactured by any electronics group.

What can computers do – and what will they never be able to do?

The question asked at the beginning has still not been answered: what could the first computers do, and – more importantly – what can computers do today?

The first instructions that the Zuse 1, for example, could process were something like 'add 0 and 1' or 'subtract 5 from 6'. There is nothing particularly revolutionary about that but these operations could at least be carried out incredibly quickly.

The first tasks were simple arithmetical calculations that every first-year primary schoolchild can easily work out and that were a long way from being really useful.

As computers became increasingly quick and powerful, new and more demanding tasks could be assigned to the electronic assistants. Computers could now collect data and use it to manage a list of customers, for example. They could also edit text and were, therefore, far more flexible than any typewriter. These are only two areas in which a computer can be used.

The following overview shows which tasks a computer can undertake today.

Arial		▼ 10
E16		▼
	A	B
1		£23.00
2		£34.00
3		£39.60
4	Total:	£96.60
5		

1 **Computers can calculate and work out sums** Besides simple arithmetic operations (adding, multiplying etc.) a modern computer is also proficient in complex mathematical operations, including sines, root extraction, squares and calculation of interest.

Customers

Surname	First name	Title	First Purchase
Marks	Mike	Mr	05.06.1989
Andrews	Richard	Mr	07.09.1995
Harris	Graeme	Dr	04.06.1996
Jameson	Valerie	Miss	01.03.1997
Holland	Daniel	Mr	17.04.1992

2 Computers can manage data in a structured way

They can manage a list of regular customers as well as an inventory. Databases also contain arithmetic operations, for example, the adding up of stocks.

File   Edit   View   Insert   Format   Tools   Table   Window

Dear Sir,

Thank you for your letter of 22nd May.

This is to confirm that we are happy with the details you have provided and we look forward to speaking to you soon.

3 Computers can edit text

Text entered using a keyboard can be filed on a disk, added to or amended if required and used time and again.

4 Computers can work with graphics and photographs

Photographs can be read into the computer and edited there. Colour graphics (e.g. company logos) can be created.

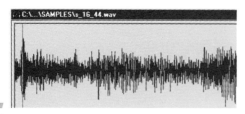

5 Computers can edit audio data

Computers can record music, voice and sounds in a similar way as cassette recorders do, but unlike the latter can also change them. So, for example, reverberation and echo can be added or certain sequences erased.

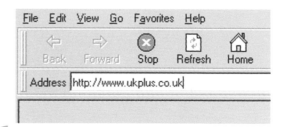

6 Computers are communicative

Computers can contact other computers in other places in the world in a matter of seconds over the 'Internet', the world-wide information superhighway, and exchange data with them, for example.

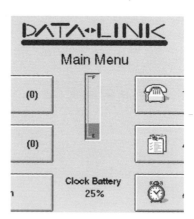

7 Computers can measure, control and regulate

A computer can, for example, record and calculate weather data and output it in the form of a weather map. It can control a production line in a factory and regulate road traffic via a control system.

So is a computer a bit like an 'electronic marvel' or a 'do-it-all'? Computers can certainly calculate, but they are 'stupid'. All operations go through a fixed program schema (algorithm) and were programmed into the computer by a person. Whenever a computer has to make decisions that cannot be included in an algorithm, people are required.

A computer can, for example, assist a doctor but cannot perform medical operations. It can make a database available to a lawyer but cannot represent his clients in criminal proceedings. Attempts to let the computer drive a car have also come to nothing so far.

Even simple processes represent an almost insurmountable obstacle for multimillion-dollar computers. The recognition of human speech, for example, is only possible with great effort and even then is unreliable. The conversion of handwriting is also a real challenge for modern computers and development engineers.

In conclusion: You are far superior to your computer, but it can relieve you of recurring routine and administrative tasks.

How a computer 'thinks': the IPO principle

In principle a computer works like a human being. This is understandable for, after all, the computer has been designed by humans and so uses them as a model.

Data processing is made up of three separate steps and this process is known as the IPO principle. IPO are the first letters of the individual steps: input, processing and output.

31

Keyboard, mouse, special readers
During the first step data must be entered into the computer. Even humans must first absorb information; for example through the eyes or ears. A computer receives information through input devices, in particular through the keyboard or special readers.

1 Input

Processor, memory
The second step processes the data. Even the human brain processes data and can do calculations or remember dates. The computer's processing unit – its brain as it were – is called a processor.

2 Processing

Printer, monitor, hard disk
During the third and final step the computer produces the result for you. The 'output device' of a human is mainly speech, as well as facial expressions, gestures and written language. The computer outputs data to the monitor or printer.

3 Output

Analog and digital: two worlds meet

Imagine you can hear music. The sound reaches your ear carried by waves – sound waves therefore transport information. The whole of nature uses waves for all types of transmission. Besides sound waves, the sunlight surrounding you is made up of waves, with each colour connected with a 'different kind' of wave. Looking and listening therefore – two of the fundamental ways we communicate – operate by waves.

Even the first computers worked with analog signals. The individual components communicated via waves. Even after the first experiments with these systems it emerged that analog signals are not suitable for the computer-controlled processing of information. Instead of clear, unambiguous states waves could also include intermediate states; there are no end of intermediate stages between the 'very loud' and 'very quiet' stages of a sound wave, for example 'medium loud'.

If information is transmitted in the form of waves, we talk about an analog signal.

A computer can work far better and quicker with discrete information. All modern computers store data in the form of two states only: 'off' and 'on', or 'zero' and 'one'.

If information is characterised by just two different states, we talk about a digital signal.

So two completely different worlds meet: the analog world of man and the digital world of the electronic computer.

If a continuous analog signal is to be converted into digital information the analog wave is split into small segments. For each individual segment the computer decides from a threshold value whether the state is 'one' or 'zero'. The result is a machine-readable digital format.

33

An analog signal can be translated into a digital signal. This type of translator is called an analog-to-digital converter and is of central importance for the whole computer world. A digital-to-analog converter does the opposite.

Man can make contact with a computer and give it instructions through an analog-to-digital converter. Your computer communicates in the other direction with you via a digital-to-analog converter.

We can use an example to show a typical application in which digital signals are converted into analog signals. A recorded piece of music is to be edited on the computer and then reproduced over the computer's speakers.

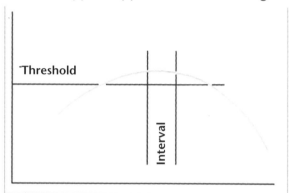

1 **Recording the piece of music**
The music is recorded as an audio signal, for example using a microphone. The signal exists as an analog signal.

2 **Conversion into a digital signal**
As the computer can only work with digital signals an analog-to-digital converter translates the music into a digital signal. The translation takes only a fraction of a second.

3 Processing the music

You can now process the music using your computer, e.g. alter the loudness level, erase sequences or add an echo effect.

4 Reconversion into an analog signal

So that the speaker can reproduce the music a digital-to-analog converter translates the (altered) music back into an analog signal.

5 Reproducing the piece of music

The analog signal is reproduced through the speakers of your computer.

The technical process of converting 'analog into digital' and vice versa is very complex and involves problems caused by this principle. Because the analog wave is sampled at certain intervals deterioration occurs. With cheap analog-to-digital converters an audible hiss, for example, is recorded which comes from the conversion.

Incidentally, digital technology arrived in other areas of daily life a long time ago. Your digital watch does not use hands to show the time, but numbers. Audio CDs do not record music as waves but use digital signals.

35

Short-term and long-term memory

How does a computer 'remember' data? You know that, according to the IPO principle, processing requires the input of data. A computer can file away any information permanently or temporarily and process it when required.

The standardised filing of any information is called 'storing'. The reading of stored information is the opposite of storing and is called 'loading'.

The computer's memory can also be compared with the human brain. If you look in the telephone directory to get the telephone number of a business partner you remember the combination of numbers. You call up the number, have your conversation, and already you have forgotten the number.

The brain's short-term memory can store data and make it available for a short period of time. However, the data filed away here quickly fades away and is then erased. The computer also has a short-term memory like this.

Memories that can only store information for a short time are called temporary memories.

You know your best friend's telephone number without having to look it up. Even after many years you have not forgotten the date of your partner's birthday, and you do not have to refer to a notepad for the number of your house. Clearly the brain works with a long-term memory that can store information in the form of memory for an indefinite time.

Memories that
can store
information
indefinitely are
called
permanent
memories.

If, in the above example, you call the telephone number you did not know, the times the process known as 'remembering' starts. You remember the telephone number, and perhaps after you have called it five or six times you know the number off by heart.

Here, a piece of information was transferred from the short-term memory to the long-term memory; a process which your computer is also able to perform.

Is there really no time limit on the information as the definition claims? Go back to the example above. If you have not called a particular telephone number for a while you start to forget it. Was it 45589 or 45859? The longer the period of time the less you remember the number.

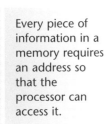

Every piece of
information in a
memory requires
an address so
that the
processor can
access it.

American studies have shown that the brain never forgets information and once information has been stored it is available for life. What we know as 'forgetting' is more the loss of data paths which doctors know as 'engrams'. If, by chance, you activate one of these data paths forgotten information is suddenly available again – you know this by the term *déjà vu*.

Admittedly, your computer does not experience *déjà vu*, but even it recognises data paths to information that is stored away permanently. To request information for processing the processor needs an address under which the information was stored. If the address is missing the data is still stored but lost de facto because the address cannot be obtained.

A computer's means of transport is called a bus system, or 'bus' for short.

When the processor requests information the data has to reach the processor by means of a transport system. The 'information superhighway' in your computer connects all the components and transports information between them.

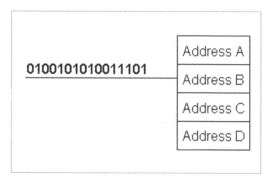

0100101010011101	Address A
	Address B
	Address C
	Address D

The language of the computer: binary format

Why is the human numbering system based on the number 10? The decimal system, as it is called, has its origins in the number of fingers. Our forefathers added and subtracted using their fingers to help them.

1	→	**1**
56	→	**111000**
234	→	**11101010**

The binary system is the number system every computer uses and only recognises two digits: one and zero.

If the computer only recognises the two states of 'one' and 'zero', which number format is it using? It will work with a number system that takes account of this peculiarity.

In fact every decimal number can be expressed as a binary number. The binary number is a string of zeros and ones; for us humans these numbers are almost incomprehensible. Fortunately the computer undertakes the conversion and so saves you the laborious task. You can, therefore, input the arithmetical operation 'add 50 and 50' into your computer in plain text and obtain '100' as the result. The computer has, however, calculated this, invisible to and hidden from you, using binary numbers.

What's in
this chapter?

You will understand what happens between
switching on the PC and the start of the
graphical user interface. You will see that your
computer carries out a test on itself whenever it
is switched on and indicates errors.

We also tell you what an operating system is
and why it has
a 'kernel'.

Finally we
explain the
purpose of a
driver and
how it is
integrated.

Shut Down Windows

Are you sure you want to:

⦿ Shut down the computer?

○ Restart the computer?

○ Restart the computer in MS-DOS mode?

○ Close all programs and log on as a different user?

Your already know:

Your are going to learn about:

41

The start-up process made transparent

You switch your computer on, and a few minutes later you are presented with the usual desktop: if you are working with a modern computer, Windows 95, for example, is started up; users of older systems must make do with more spartan interfaces such as MS-DOS.

Except for a couple of status messages, the fact that the PC carries out numerous important tasks in the few minutes it is starting up is hidden from sight. Nevertheless in this short period of time **essential operations** are carried out without which your computer would not start-up – often called 'power up' in computer jargon.

The proper starting up of the computer is called **powering up**.

The functions your computer carries out in detail are more than just interesting. Messages that are given during startup indicate **machine errors** and so help prevent data losses before you start work.

Switching off is also particularly important. Not 'shutting down' the computer properly can result in loss of data, and in addition your system can be damaged.

Shutting down means finishing working with the computer properly.

A brief summary at the beginning of this chapter lists the tasks your computer performs. The other steps in this chapter show you in detail what happens after switching on.

At the end of the chapter we explain why you cannot simply switch off the computer, but must first shut it down.

1 You press the 'power' switch on your computer.

A power unit built into your computer supplies all the components of the system with power. So the hard disk, for example, rotates with a noticeable whirr.

2 The computer starts a special self-test routine.

A **routine** always contains recurrent information that can be understood and processed by the computer.

By means of the self-test routine the computer checks that the most important systems are functioning correctly and also detects errors.

3 The computer reads information from a permanent memory.

System settings, for example relating to the size of your hard disk or other hardware, are read in the third step.

4 The computer loads basic routines.

Some routines that are imperative for the operation of the computer are loaded into a memory.

43

5 The computer loads the operating system.

> Windows 95, OS/2 or another operating system is loaded on top of the basic routines.

6 Configuration files are loaded from the operating system.

> Special files adapt the operating system to the hardware

On starting up, your computer finds information about its operating environment in a configuration file. This includes, for example, the language in which your PC is to communicate with you or currency and date formats.

7 The graphical interface is loaded.

> Finally, the well-known Windows 95 interface, for example, is displayed. Finished!

Self-test: the POST routine

When the power is switched on a **special routine** is run. This small program is called the **POST routine** (Power On Self Test) and is stored in a permanent memory.

The **POST routine** carries out a self-test on the most important components of the PC and so ensures they function correctly.

This program generates a sequence of codes which the PC interprets internally. If, for example, it is established that the floppy disk drive is not working properly the POST routine returns 'Floppy Disk Drive Failure'. If no errors are detected the PC receives the error code 00 and continues the start-up process.

If your computers dealer have their own workshop, they can access the error code using special **diagnostic hardware** and determine the cause of the error even if the PC can no longer output the message itself.

Certainly numerous errors can be detected by the POST routine; however, successful completion of the test does not guarantee that your system is actually working completely free of errors.

ROM

The personal computer is an **open system**, which means that its individually integrated components can vary greatly.

You certainly know the principle from buying your PC: your dealer will have asked you whether you wanted the hard drive to contain one or two gigabytes, how big the working memory was to be and what graphics card should be installed in the computer.

How does your computer 'know' which **hard drive** was installed or how many megabytes of **main memory** are available? Another interesting question is, how your PC can remember the **date and time** even when you disconnect its power supply.

A permanent memory or **ROM** (read only memory) contains information which the PC manufacturer programmed in during production. Every time it is switched on, the PC accesses the ROM and reads out information. The POST routine, which varies greatly depending on your computer's equipment, is also stored in the ROM.

The name 'ROM' refers to the fact that information from this memory can only be read, there is no write access. It stands for 'read only memory'. A ROM does not require power to retain the programmed information. Even after several years with no power supply, data can be read out of the ROM without any of it being lost.

It all sounds very logical and is easy to understand. What happens, though, if your PC is supplied with another hard drive or more main memory is installed? A small memory segment is closely linked with the ROM, however it can store certain parameters.

This memory is called **CMOS** and carries data to your hard drive or to the equipment of the main memory, for example. Other individual configurations are also stored in the CMOS.

So that the data remains stored when the power is switched off the computer has a small **buffer battery** in the form of an accumulator. The accumulator supplies the CMOS with energy and also allows the clock and date to continue to operate when the PC is switched off.

When your computer is started up, information is first loaded from the ROM and then supplied with data from the CMOS.

If your PC has not been switched on for **four or five months** it can happen that the PC will start up with an error message and the operating system will not be loaded. The error message 'CMOS Setup Checksum Error' is a typical symptom of a run-down buffer battery, the consequence of which is missing information from the CMOS memory.

WHAT'S THIS?

If you do not want to use your PC for several months you should still switch it on at monthly intervals for about half an hour. In this way the built-in buffer battery will be recharged.

Your computer now no longer 'knows' which hard drive and working memory are installed and that is why it refuses to co-operate.

RAM

WHAT'S THIS?

RAM is the abbreviation for 'random access memory'. It only stores information when the power is on.

Your PC has another memory: the RAM or 'main memory'.

Compared with the ROM the RAM is much quicker, but can only store information while the PC is switched on.

As the name 'main memory' suggests, this type of memory plays a central role. All information is stored in it and inputted data is kept in it temporarily. When the computer is switched on. the ROM can transfer speed-sensitive elements into the faster RAM.

Because information is lost when the PC is switched off, long-term memories are necessary. We shall explain the main differences in a later chapter.

The BIOS: the computer's brain

Let's look a little more closely at the start-up process of a PC. So far a self-test has been carried out, information loaded from a permanent memory, and data accessed in a configuration memory.

The basic settings are therefore available; what is missing is a routine which makes it possible to access the most important components of the PC. How, for example, is the PC to know at that time where the operating system is?

Programs that are particularly machine-intimate are also contained in the ROM. An instruction stored here could, for example, read: 'Command to hard drive: store the user's document in the area sector 3/track 4'. We shall explain later what exactly sectors and tracks are; in short, the afore-mentioned routine communicates directly with the hardware.

The BIOS controls machine-intimate access and is loaded before the operating system.

Because this program is so closely connected with basic tasks it is called **BIOS** (basic input–output system). It is part of the programs stored in the ROM and is run before the operating system is loaded.

Boot sector and operating system

After the information has been loaded from ROM and CMOS your PC loads the **operating system**.

The concept of an operating system pervades the computer media and you will certainly have come across it when you bought your computer. You will know from the dealer's brochure, if you did not already know, that Windows 95 is one such operating system.

An operating system gives instructions direct to the BIOS and so forms an **interface**, as it were, between you and the hardware. Whereas your computer's BIOS communicates directly with the hardware, an order from the operating system in the schema reads for example: 'Instruction to BIOS: write the user's document to the hard disk'. The translation into tracks and sectors is handled by the BIOS.

An **operating system** is an interface between the user and hardware. It makes it possible, for example, to work with printers and disks.

Current operating systems can, however, do much more. For example, they provide their user with a graphical interface that can be operated with the mouse, they organise and check disks and can run several programs at once. We shall describe some of these in more detail in later chapters of this book.

So that all the instructions you give the hardware (e.g. 'Print my document') are carried out, the operating system must be continuously present. Once the operating system is loaded it will be there until the computer is shut down and switched off. It is run in the background,so to speak, while you as the user create a letter with Word for Windows or graphics with Corel Draw in the foreground.

Resident programs are permanently available in the background after loading. Operating systems are always resident.

The technical term for this permanent presence is **resident**. The operating system is a resident program because it is run in the background.

How does the BIOS know which operating system you want to load? After all, you may use an alternative operating system to Windows 95, such as OS/2.

Instead of a statement 'I use Windows' your computer does not recognise the **type of operating system**. On starting up, the operating system is searched for in an **absolute area** of the hard drive (or even floppy disk) and information found there is assumed to belong to the operating system.

This defined area on the disk is called the **boot sector** and always contains the operating system. 'Booting' is a slang expression for powering up a computer. The BIOS loads this absolute sector and interprets the data stored there as the operating system.

Computer viruses which lodge in this area of the PC are particularly dangerous. They are loaded directly when the PC is powered up and can then carry out their destructive work.

Naturally there is not room for the whole of the operating system in the very small boot sector. Only a small part is loaded at that time. It is known as the **kernel** and carries out the most basic functions of an operating system.

Configuration files and installation

So that the operating system can be adapted to your computer, many programs copy individual files to your hard disk.

If you buy a new **computer mouse**, for example, this comes with a disk which must be 'installed' after the mouse has been connected.

A **driver** forms the basis for the integration of a new component into an existing computer system. Drivers are special files that are transferred to your hard disk during installation.

These files, which are transferred to the hard disk during installation, contain information about the new component and instructions for the operating system which define the way the new components are to be handled. In technical jargon this type of **control file** is also called a **driver** or 'hardware driver'.

However, during installation not only are files copied but the operating system is adapted to the modified conditions.

So-called **configuration files** form the basis for adapting your computer. Each modification to the configuration is recorded in one of these files which are, therefore, very **dynamic**.

In a way the CMOS is also a type of configuration file. However it is not part of the operating system but loaded before this.

A **configuration file** contains information about the individual components and the operating system's own equipment.

51

The type and structure of the configuration files used depends exclusively on the operating system. Several files can supplement each other and each takes account of a certain configuration.

Such a configuration file can, for example, contain the following type of entry: 'This computer is installed with a Logitech pilot computer mouse. On switching on, the correct driver must first be loaded'. So that you can get an impression of how such information appears in computer language the next line shows the actual entry in the configuration file:

DEVICE=C:\CONFIG\LOGITECH.SYS

Other programs have also 'discovered' this practical type of file for themselves. Word for Windows and Corel Draw also create a configuration file during installation.

There are two typical configuration files that exist under **Microsoft operating systems,** including MS DOS, Windows 95 and Windows NT. The file called **CONFIG.SYS** is supplemented by a second configuration file, the **AUTOEXEC.BAT.**

In addition, windows systems operate with a configuration file that is used internally within Windows and called **WIN.INI,** which and is connected with particular tasks and functions.

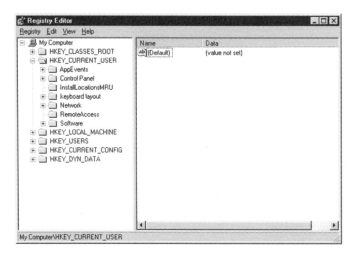

WHAT'S THIS?

The **registry database** is a special form of the configuration file which is particularly powerful.

Over and above this Windows 95 and Windows NT 4.0 use a **registry database** which is a more modern form of the configuration file.

To take a typical example, the following pages show you how a supplied hardware driver is installed and the Windows registry database is adapted accordingly. If you want to install a driver yourself you can follow the steps below.

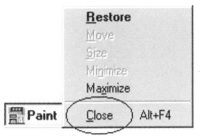

1 Close all programs that are open, because occasionally the system can crash when a driver is being installed.

2 Click the START button, and point to SETTINGS. Click CONTROL PANEL, and select the *Add New Hardware* icon.

53

3 The 'Add New Hardware Wizard' will appear. Confirm the window by clicking *Next*.

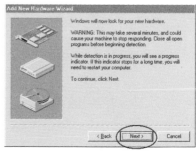

4 Windows 95 asks you if new hardware is to be installed. Confirm this by clicking *Next*. You can also confirm the following warning message.

5 While new hardware is being detected a progress bar shows the course of the installation process.

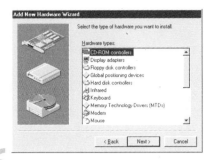

6 The hardware categories are listed so that the driver can be assigned to a component.

7 After installation the device is ready for use and can be used under Windows 95.

Start-up of the graphical interface

After the kernel and all the necessary drivers have been loaded the **graphical interface** of the operating system is loaded. A typical example is Windows 95 which, although it can certainly work without a graphical interface, loads the usual desktop as standard after the PC is powered up.

55

Whereas the configuration files AUTOEXEC.BAT and CONFIG.SYS were loaded earlier, the **registry database** is only accessed at this point. From the entries, the driver that is responsible for the screen output and activates your printer driver, is loaded.

Shutting down the operating system: exiting the operation

A **bad mistake** made by beginners which can unfortunately lead to serious system errors, is switching off the computer without first **shutting down** the operating system properly.

Why is it so important that you don't just switch off the system? Earlier **DOS versions** were far less sensitive and did not have any functions that would have had an allergic reaction to being switched off. The whole of the DOS operating system occupied a fraction of the space in the working memory required by Windows 95.

On start-up, important system functions of the operating system are loaded into the working memory. As it is an **intelligent** operating system, you the user do not see it operating. While for example, you are typing text in the foreground using Word for Windows, Windows 95 may be carrying out a **maintenance process** in the background unnoticed by you.

It would be **fatal** if you were to save your Word text and then switch off your PC. The maintenance process in the background would be immediately interrupted and might result in **loss of data**.

Users of older DOS versions always knew what their computer was doing. If Word for DOS was started up there was no such maintenance process running in the background. With the increasing integration of powerful functions and, above all, the possibility of being able to run several processes in parallel the risk of an operating error also increased.

In some cases you cannot prevent the computer being switched off unintentionally. During a **power failure** or if you accidentally knock the POWER switch on your PC with your leg, the PC is not shut down properly.

Power failures that occur while a document is being saved or during other write operations are particularly dangerous and feared by the user. A file that may only be half-saved is **worthless** to the computer and besides is no longer even half-readable. Although the file has, therefore, become unusable it is, nevertheless, occupying memory space on the hard disk.

In this case you should, above all, perform a **routine check** on your computer's disks. This check detects and deletes **damaged files** so that the hard disk memory which was identified as being occupied before is available again.

Windows 95 and Windows NT, for example, provide a **diagnostic program** called **ScanDisk** which can repair minor hard disk errors. Newer revisions of Windows 95 detect that a system has not been closed down and automatically check the local hard disks during the next start-up.

The following steps show you how a hard disk check is run. We have used Windows 95 as an example but appropriate **system tools** are available for all the more **modern operating systems**, including Windows NT, Apple Macintosh and OS/2.

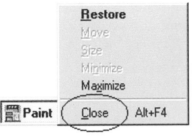

1 Before you begin the task, close all programs that are still open, because errors can occur during the check which may lead to a system crash.

2 Click the START button, and point to PROGRAMS. In the menu which appears point to ACCESSORIES and then SYSTEM TOOLS. The hard disk checking program can now be called by clicking *ScanDisk*.

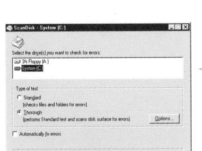

3 In the *'Select the drive you want to check for errors list'*, select the 'hard disk label (C:)' and confirm by clicking *Start*.

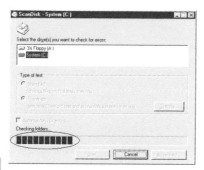

4 A progress bar shows you the course of the hard disk check.

5 An error report indicates any errors detected and any additional data about your hard disk.

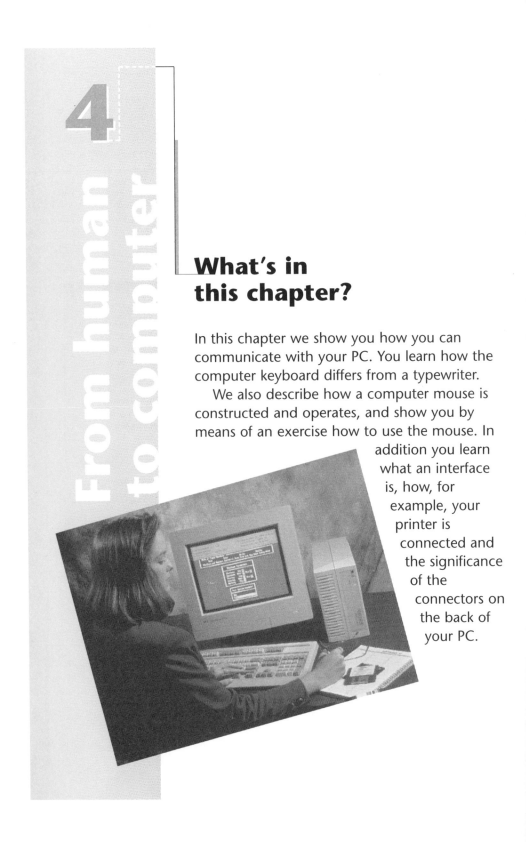

4

From human to computer

What's in this chapter?

In this chapter we show you how you can communicate with your PC. You learn how the computer keyboard differs from a typewriter.

We also describe how a computer mouse is constructed and operates, and show you by means of an exercise how to use the mouse. In addition you learn what an interface is, how, for example, your printer is connected and the significance of the connectors on the back of your PC.

Your already know:

Your are going to learn about:

Communicating with the PC

A still unfulfilled dream of computer specialists is **voice-controlled communication with computer systems**. A futuristic, early morning scenario from the year 2000 (such systems will have become a reality by then) could look like this:

Still half-asleep and with your eyes only half-open you go into the kitchen. A steaming hot cup of coffee should get rid of the tiredness from your limbs, so you give your household computer the **voice instruction**: 'Make coffee for one'.

With your cup of coffee in your hand you tune into the latest electronic edition of your daily newspaper. There are no sheets of paper; instead you make yourself comfortable in your armchair and instruct your computer: 'Next page'.

After you have arrived at your office and switched on your computer you empty your (naturally **electronic**) **mailbox**. A letter from an old college friend, who is abroad at the moment, catches your eye. 'Display letter from Michael.' You **dictate to your computer a letter** several pages long for your friend which is then sent automatically.

Admittedly this scene is still pie in the sky at the moment. Dictation systems certainly do already exist which can take down **complete texts**. The 'VoiceType' developed by IBM, for example, is considerably well developed and allows the user to dictate whole texts allowing for some peculiarities. Recognition of continuous speech is, however, expecting too much even of modern computer systems.

You can communicate conventionally in various ways with your PC. You already know that devices for doing this are grouped together under the collective term **'input devices'**. On the following pages you will become acquainted with the main input devices and learn how to use them.

Interfaces: the door to the outside

Follow the cable that connects your computer mouse with the case of your computer. Usually, the connecting cable ends at a plug connector at the back of the case.

Now pull out the connector after having loosened the securing screws by hand. If you take the trouble to count the pins (contacts) on the mouse connector you will discover that there are exactly nine of them. Each of these pins carries **certain information** either from or to the computer. Naturally, it has to be specified precisely which signal is carried by which pin so that your mouse, for example, can communicate with your PC.

A **connector–socket combination** like this is called an **interface**. Very different devices can be connected at an interface, allowing your PC to be expanded. One unit that is obviously connected to an interface like this is the mouse.

An **interface** connects external devices via a standard plug connector with the computer.

Although there are a vast number of different interfaces, four are sufficient for your PC. Because each interface is fitted with a different socket and has a different number of pins there is no risk of confusing them. You can try this out by seeing if the mouse will go in a different socket on your PC.

Every PC is supplied with the following interfaces as standard:

1 **9-pin serial interface**
The mouse, for example, is operated via this interface. Because the interface only has nine pins the appropriate connector is very narrow.

2 25-pin serial interface

The 25-pin serial interface is much
wider than the 9-pin one. A
modem is usually connected here.

3 25-pin parallel interface

The parallel interface always
connects the printer with the PC.
Some external disks also
communicate via the parallel
interface.

4 15-pin game interface

If you want to connect a joystick to
your computer to control games the
game interface is used.

How do the various types of interface differ from each other? The
two **serial interfaces** are compatible with each other, so can be used
for the same tasks. So a 9-pin mouse can also be connected to the
25-pin serial interface if an appropriate adaptor is used.

All interfaces are one of the two types
'parallel' and 'serial'.

Information that is sent via a **serial interface**
reaches the receiver only gradually. To
illustrate this, imagine a **single-lane road**,
where the vehicles travelling along it are the
data. The vehicles (data) move one after
another (in a series). For this reason a serial
interface is not particularly quick, but it is
robust and not prone to interference. It is
very suitable for **transferring
small amounts of data**, such
as that supplied by the
mouse.

$\longleftarrow$ 01001010

The **serial interface** sends only one unit of information at a time. Larger amounts of data must be sent one after another.

Larger amounts of data are sent via a **parallel interface**. Your PC's parallel interface, for example, extends the single lane of the serial interface by seven. In total, **eight units of information** can be transferred at a time, which explains the high transfer rate. Your printer, for instance, receives a lot of data at once, so that you don't have to wait long for your printout. Many time-critical actions are therefore carried out via the parallel interface.

The standard **parallel interface** of a PC carries eight units of information at the same time and so is much faster than a serial interface.

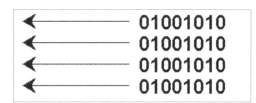

In addition to the printer, many other devices are also operated via the parallel interface, such as **external disks** or **network cards** for portable computers.

You may be surprised that the parallel interface connector has up to 25 pins, but only eight data bits are sent at once. As only one wire is required to send one unit of information, 17 pins seem superfluous.

So what are these extra pins for? The contact pins numbered 14 to 25, for example, are actually short-circuited to each other and form the ground. Some contacts are unoccupied and form a reserve for separate projects.

WHAT'S THIS?

Besides data, **status signals** are also sent via the interface and convey information about the operating status of the device connected.

The remaining pins carry **status messages**, which for example a printer returns to the PC. This is how the PC 'knows' that the printer is 'online' or is out of paper. These **status signals** are very important and are transmitted at the same time as the actual data.

WHAT'S THIS?

A serial data cable should be no longer than 6 to 8 metres, a parallel cable no longer than 5 metres.

The **length of a connecting cable** is very important for the correct transfer of data. Instead of the business letter you want your printer may only print out gobbledegook. A typical cause of this is a cable which is too long and which degrades the signals being carried. To avoid such errors the cables should be as **short as possible**.

WHAT'S THIS?

USB stands for **universal serial bus** and is a new interface system which the manufacturers hope will eliminate the cable and standards chaos.

An end to the **interface chaos** may already be in sight. Various manufacturers, including the PC giant Siemens-Nixdorf, have designed a revolutionary system called **USB** (universal serial bus). In future, PCs will be fitted with this interface system and the user will no longer be burdened with technical details, such as different ports, connectors and cable lengths.

Instead, the PC case, keyboard and monitor will have several sockets to which you can connect any equipment. You can choose to couple the computer mouse to the keyboard or to the monitor without the result being any different. In addition the serial data will be able to be transferred much more quicklyr than is the case with present systems.

Other connectors

When you looked for and hopefully found the parallel and serial connectors on the back of your PC you would certainly have noticed numerous other connectors. This is a good opportunity to tell you about them.

The power outlet

In the introductory chapter we explained that your PC is connected to the mains with a normal mains cable which ends at the power supply.

The power supply transmits mains voltage to an outlet at the back of your PC case. The monitor can be connected here. This is both useful and practical because when the computer is switched on the monitor is also supplied with power and so does not have to be switched on separately.

The monitor connector

A noticeably thick cable with a 15-pin socket is permanently attached to the monitor. This cable conveys all the information about the picture to be displayed to the monitor. Because the information transported is extremely sensitive to external interference, which would reduce the picture quality, the cable is heavily **protecte**d.

Audio sockets

If your PC has audio facilities, you will have discovered some other connectors at the back of the computer case. Small, round sockets transmit **audio signals** to connected **stereo equipment** or jukeboxes. In addition, sound sources such as a cassette recorder or microphone can be connected.

67

Audio sockets are usually stereo-capable and are marked black (left channel) and red (right channel) in accordance with marking used in audio technology.

External SCSI connector

Some PCs are fitted with a wide, 40-pin external SCSI connector. We will explain all about SCSI is in a later chapter. Special external devices are operated via this connector, for example a **scanner** to optically **'read in'** graphics, photographs and text.

The network socket

If you operate your PC on a network you will also find a network connector. As there are a great many different types of network connectors within the PC industry there is no generally supplied network socket.

The online connector

If, when you bought your PC, you got an ISDN adapter or an internal modem you will find another connector. It connects your computer to the telephone socket or to your ISDN connection.

The keyboard: input device number one

'The' input device is the **keyboard**. You can probably use it quite intuitively because you know the keyboard layout from the **typewriter**.

If you learnt the **10-finger system** on a normal typewriter you will have to pick up new keys and key combinations. Interestingly, it is common to discover that even people who use a PC at work for administrative tasks do not know the functions of all the keys.

The PC keyboard differs from a standard typewriter keyboard in that it has **several extra keys**. In total it has 102 keys including a number of special keys required to **control special functions**, which can in part be specified individually by you.

A keyboard of this type is described as a MF-II keyboard. This standard is used by all manufacturers and guarantees that you can also find your way around a colleague's PC.

MF-II keyboards have 102 keys. MF is the abbreviation for 'multifunction' and refers to the fact that a PC keyboard provides more functions than a typewriter keyboard.

Unfortunately, as you learnt in the previous chapters, the computer world is anything but homogeneous. It is almost a miracle that manufacturers have not designed their own keyboard but have kept to the MF-II standard.

Outside the PC world, however, **key chaos** reigns. If you get the opportunity to look at the keyboard of a Macintosh or Amiga computer you will see **considerable differences** from the PC architecture. Both types of computer certainly contain the letter keypad, but all the other keys are laid out differently as well as being defined differently and labelled accordingly.

Take a look at the keyboard of your PC. The letter area begins with the keys **Q-W-E-R-T-Y**, and so this type of keyboard is also called a **QWERTY keyboard**. Other keyboards have a different layout but still comply with the MF-II standard.

Keyboards with the
English layout of
letters are called
QWERTY keyboards.

In this section we shall familiarise you with all the keys on a modern computer keyboard and show you how you can use them in your daily tasks.

Codepages prevent code chaos

How does the computer know whether you have connected an **English keyboard** or a different one? The answer is, it doesn't know! If you connect a German keyboard, for example, to your PC, pressing the 'Z' key will produce a 'Y' on the screen.

Understandably that is not desirable. A special table integrated in the operating system called '**Codepage**' contains country-specific information. So umlauts and the ß are available to German users and a French person can use accented vowels.

A **codepage** contains country-specific information. It is loaded when the operating system is started up and remains in the background while you are working.

When the operating system is started up the appropriate codepage is loaded so that you have the right keyboard layout.

Codepages, therefore, make a PC extremely flexible.

Connection to the PC

Firstly, look at the cable connecting the keyboard with the PC. There are five pins and, because of notches, the round connector cannot be put in the socket the wrong way round. On some makes, a **small white arrow** on one side of the connector indicates the top.

If the cable is too short you can buy a spiral extension cable for around £5 in a specialist shop.

Some makes of computer are supplied with much smaller connectors which do not work with the standard format. These connectors are called 'PS/2 keyboard connectors' because the manufacturer, IBM, first used this type of connector in its PS/2 series. Portable computers (**notebooks**) in particular are fitted with PS/2 keyboard connectors for reasons of space.

If you want to use a standard keyboard on a computer with a PS/2 connector you will have to buy an appropriate adapter.

Setting up the keyboard

On the bottom of the keyboard you will find two **fold-out feet**, with which you can tilt the keyboard to achieve the most comfortable position.

A small switch on the bottom of some keyboards is marked 'AT/XT'. Earlier XT generation computers worked with a different keyboard layout that was not compatible with modern computers.

This switch allows your keyboard to be set to the old XT standard. Today this is no longer of any significance; the switch is the relic from bygone computer times.

There is an important reason why we mention this switch: jokers like to use the XT switch to drive the unsuspecting PC beginner to despair. If the PC does not detect the keyboard when it is switched on because the switch is set incorrectly the start-up process will be aborted with an error message: '**keyboard failure**'. Who looks *under* the keyboard?

Finding your way around the keyboard

The main input area corresponds to the typewriter keyboard. You input your text and simple number combinations using the alphanumeric part of the keyboard.

Above the keys used for inputting data you will find twelve keys numbered F1 to F12. These are function keys and are divided into three blocks of four.

At the top left is the Esc key and to the right of the function keys you will find three other keys: Print , Scroll Lock and Pause .

The right-hand part of the keyboard contains the numeric keypad which corresponds to the adding machine layout. Each key has a second function as well as that of a number or an operand.

Between the alphanumeric and number keys you will find four arrow keys, and above these are another six keys.

The input keys

You use the alphanumeric keys to input text. Speed typists will appreciate that the 'F' and 'J' keys feel slightly different to the rest. On some keyboard models these keys are **slightly narrower**, on other designs they are **raised**. This makes it easier to find your way around, particularly when touch-typing using the ten-finger system.

As with typewriters, upper-case, or capital letters can be produced by holding down the Shift key and selecting the corresponding letter.

If you have to type longish sections in upper case, for example headings, you can use the Caps Lock key. A green LED on the right-hand part of the keyboard shows that the Caps Lock key is on. To return to normal mode, press the Caps Lock key again.

Symbols marked as the third character on keys can be selected by holding down the Alt Gr key and pressing the relevant key. So, for example, the ¶ symbol can be reproduced using the key combination Alt Gr + ~ .

The Enter key

The Return or Enter key on the computer corresponds to the 'carriage return' on a typewriter. It is located on the right-hand side of the input keys and is conspicuous as it is the largest key.

In literature and program documentation you will find both the terms 'Enter' and 'Return'. Both names refer to the same key; in this book we use 'Enter'.

73

Generally you execute a command and send it to the operating system using the Enter key. If, for example, you tell your computer that you want to erase your hard disk it will only do this when you have confirmed it with the Enter key.

The Enter key can have other functions; for example, in word processing pressing this key ends a paragraph in your text document, like a carriage return.

The numeric keypad

If you want to enter large columns of numbers you can use the numeric keypad.

It is difficult to understand why some users hardly ever make use of the keypad. However, a frequent cause of errors lies in the fact that two functions are connected with the numeric keypad.

Besides **entering numbers**, the marked keys can also be used for **navigating** around the screen. The cursor in an electronic spreadsheet, for example, can be moved to the required position easily and without much movement of the hand.

By pressing the Num Lock key you can alternate between entering numbers and navigating with the arrows. If, therefore, a number appears on the screen instead of the required arrow movement (or vice versa) press the Num Lock key.

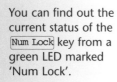

You can find out the current status of the Num Lock key from a green LED marked 'Num Lock'.

Position keys

The six position keys which are to the left of the numeric keypad can be used to **quickly position** the input marker, which in computer jargon is called the cursor.

'Cursor' is the name for the marker that shows you where text you enter will appear.

The function of the position keys is **program-dependent.**

We shall show you typical uses of the position keys.

In a word-processing program the Home key takes you back to the beginning of the line. Many spreadsheets use the Home key to go back to the beginning of the spreadsheet or line.

Likewise the End key takes you to the end of the current line. It is the 'opposite', as it were, of the Home key.

The Page Up and Page Down keys move your cursor one screen page up or down. You can, for example, use them to move through the text and scour it for any formatting errors.

75

Strictly speaking, the Insert and Delete keys do not belong to the position keys even though they are are grouped with them in a keypad. In most word-processing programs, and also in input fields in the operating system the Insert key switches into overwrite mode. In a later exercise we shall show you the importance of this mode.

The four arrow keys, which are directly below the position keys, are used to move the cursor. Their function is equivalent to that of the arrow keys on the numeric keypad.

Function keys

The **function key** area above the number row of the input keys contains twelve keys. People new to PCs who have previously typed text on a typewriter can easily confuse the top two rows on the keyboard.

Function keys perform a particular function as their name suggests. But doesn't every key do that?

More precisely, you can allocate a particular function to function keys. Function keys are, thus, user-definable.

A typical example:

If you often have to insert tables in the text which you create using a word processor you can make this work easier by using a function key. So, in Microsoft Word, for example, you can create a standard table and link it with the F12 key. Word then inserts a table ready formatted whenever you press F12.

Some function keys are specified as standard. Depending on the operating system, different **operations** are triggered. If you work with Windows 95, by pressing F1 you activate the **help function**, which answers your questions about the program.

You will learn more about the function keys later on in the book.

The Escape key

The key in the top left-hand corner of your keyboard is very important. The Escape key, marked Esc, aborts the current operation or request before it is carried out.

An example: If your computer asks you if you really want to erase all the data from your hard disk, the Esc key aborts the operation. If you activate the print function by mistake but do not want the current document on paper, Esc interrupts printing.

77

Control keys

On the bottom row of the keyboard you will find the `Ctrl`, `Alt` and `Alt Gr` keys. There are two `Ctrl` keys, one on each side.

We have already talked about the Alt Gr key, but what do the other three keys do?

'Ctrl' is the abbreviation for **Control**.

The two Control keys have the same function. There are only two of them for convenience.

The Alt key ('Alt' is the abbreviation for 'Alternative') performs a similar task to the Ctrl keys, but is independent of them. Nevertheless the Alt key is classified under the generic term 'control keys'.

When you press the `Ctrl` or `Alt` key nothing happens at first. Both keys only trigger a function in combination with an alphanumeric key. The notation `Ctrl` + `P` means, for example, that you must first hold down the `Ctrl` key and then press the `P` key.

You can carry out many standard functions quicker by using key combinations. If, for example, you want to type a word in your word-processing text in italics, you can do this by using the key combination (`Ctrl` + `I`).

Windows 95 keys

With the introduction of Windows 95 Microsoft brought out a **special keyboard** which has been specially adapted to this operating system. Windows 95 is used with a MF-II keyboard, but Microsoft promises the user increased user-friendliness when the special keyboard is used.

The first Windows 95 key is the equivalent of pressing the right mouse button. You can use it to call up a special menu which contains the most frequently used program functions. Later in this chapter we will show you the function of the right mouse button.

You can activate the Start menu with the Start key, independent of other programs that are open. The Start key, thus, corresponds to a mouse click on the Start button.

What purpose do the two special Windows 95 keys serve if both keys can be replaced by a mouse click? Perhaps it is just a marketing gimmick by Microsoft who want to sell the new type of keyboard?

When you have worked with your PC for a while and frequently use the Start menu and the menu obtained with the right mouse button (the so-called **Context** menu) you will soon appreciate the extra keys. You will find it easier when creating and **formatting long passages of text** not to have to keeping moving the mouse and taking your right hand from the keyboard.

Special keys

Three other keys are located above the position keys. You will only need these keys occasionally when you are working. They are a hangover from DOS times and have lost their importance with modern operating systems like Windows 95.

The Print Screen key produces a print out of the current screen (a 'hardcopy') in the DOS window and in DOS mode.

With the Scroll Lock key you fix the screen in such a way that the arrow keys no longer move the cursor but the text in the required direction. A green LED shows that the Scroll Lock key is on.

The Pause key pauses the current program in DOS mode; pressing it again causes the program to continue running. It does not have any effect on the status of Windows 95 programs. Some programs in DOS mode can be interrupted with the key combination Ctrl + Print Screen.

The mouse supplements the keyboard

The optimum addition to the keyboard is the **computer mouse**. It is actually more a **pointer instrument** than an input device. With the mouse you can move to any **position** on the screen and trigger the functions there using the mouse buttons.

Let's first look at how a mouse is constructed and its function.

A computer mouse consists of a **plastic housing** in which a **freely moving ball** can rotate when the mouse is moved on a firm surface. So that the mouse can move smoothly it should be moved on a special pad, the mouse mat.

The gyratory movement of the ball is converted into a signal via a switch, or through an optical process, and is sent, together with the signals of the (usually) two buttons, via a cable to the computer's serial interface.

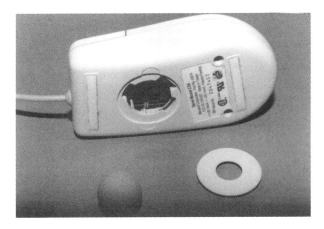

The status of the serial interface is established through a special program – **the mouse driver** – and sent to the operating system. The operating system projects a mouse pointer onto the screen, the position of which corresponds to the movements of the mouse.

Pressing one of the mouse buttons activates the required function, e.g. calls up a **menu**. Most mice have **two buttons**, but some have **three**, with the middle one only being active in special applications.

How does the left mouse button differ from the right one?

With the left mouse button you activate a function or give your computer a command. The left button is used most. If you come across the instruction 'Click . . . ' in a manual or other documentation this always refers to the left mouse button.

A **single click** selects an icon so it is ready for another action, for example the renaming or deleting of a file.

A **double-click** with the left button opens the file hidden behind an icon. The time between the two separate clicks is only a few milliseconds and most users have to practise this at first. The double-click should ensure there is a distinction between the selection and the execution of a file.

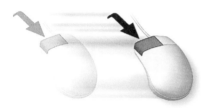

You will often be instructed to **drag** an icon or passage of text to a particular place. To do this, move the mouse onto the icon that is to be dragged, press the left button and **hold it down**. When you move the mouse now, the icon sticks

to the mouse pointer so that you can move it over the screen to a different position. When you reach this position **release** the left button to put the icon down. A file can be deleted in this way. All you have to do is drag the file icon to the **Recycle Bin**. When you release the button the file is transferred to the Recycle Bin and deleted. We'll practise dragging in a later chapter.

The function of the **right mouse button** is limited to a few special operations. In Windows environments a context-sensitive menu is available which contains commands adapted to your special requirements.

A **context-sensitive menu** contains frequently used commands which refer to the current operating mode of your software.

Does your mouse have a third button? The Microsoft specification provides for only two buttons. The middle button, if you have one, has no function in Windows environments.

The middle mouse button is only used with special software, for example for the computer-assisted creation of graphics and drawings. Certain Logitech programmes use the middle mouse button to simulate a double-click with the left mouse button.

The mouse 'sticks'

After a while it can happen that the mouse seems to 'stick'. Instead of following your movement on the mouse mat the mouse pointer does not move on the screen.

Due to the mechanical demands on the sensitive scanning switch, dust and other microscopic particles get into the housing.

In this case the **ball** and the **scanning mechanism** must be cleaned. This only takes a couple of minutes. Turn the mouse over and remove the **retaining ring** that holds the ball in the housing. Remove the ball and soak it in a **mild soap solution**. The **scanning wheels** inside the house can be clearly seen. Clean them with a cotton-wool ball that has been moistened with some **medicated alcohol**. After drying them you can put the ball, which should also be dried, back in.

Using the keyboard and mouse

Now that we have shown you in detail the meanings and functions of the numerous special keys and you know how to use the mouse you can use what you have learnt 'live'.

On the following pages we will use practical examples to guide you through using a mouse and show you the most important key combinations at work.

You can work through the examples at your PC if have with the Windows 95 or Windows NT 4.0 operating systems. Even with other interfaces the functions demonstrated work on the same principle, e.g. under OS/2 and the Unix interface X11.

Click with the left mouse button on the START button and move the mouse pointer to PROGRAMS at the top of the menu that appears. After a brief delay another menu appears to the right of the Start menu. Look for ACCESSORIES, and move the mouse pointer on to it. Click once on the *WordPad* icon with the left mouse button.

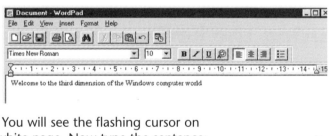

You will see the flashing cursor on the white page. Now type the sentence: - - - - - - - - - - ▶ 'Welcome to the third dimension of the Windows computer world'.

3 You can now move about in the typed text using the arrow keys. Press the ⟵ key several times, and move the cursor, using the arrow keys in the numeric keypad, to just before the word 'third'.

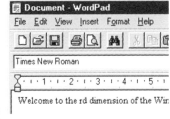

4 Your task now is to delete the first three letters of the word 'third'. To do this press the Delete key several times until 'rd' is left.

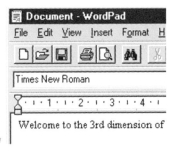

5 Now put a 3 in front of the 'rd' to complete it. Use the numeric keypad to do this, and remember to switch first into the input mode Num Lock.

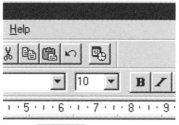

of the **Windows** computer world

6 Now highlight the word 'Windows' with the mouse. To do this click with the left mouse button in front of the 'W', hold down the left mouse button and slowly move the mouse to the right. The further you move to the right, the more letters are highlighted. When you get to the space after the word, release the mouse button and press the Delete key to delete the highlighted text.

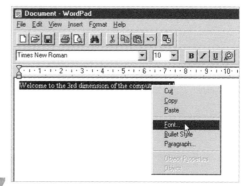

7 It is about time that the font was changed. Highlight the remaining sentence, as described in the previous step. Move the mouse pointer to any part of the highlighted area and press the right mouse button. The context menu offers you the opportunity to change the font. Try your luck, and change the font from 'Times' to 'Arial'.

8 Your task now is to embolden the words 'computer world'. First highlight the relevant words, and press the left mouse button on the 'B' button at the top.

Under the black highlighting 'computer world' appears much bolder. Click 'B' again to remove the bold font.

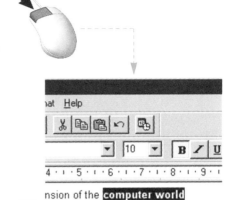

9 It's quicker with a key combination. Highlight the words 'computer world' again if you have already removed the highlighting in the previous step. Now hold the left Ctrl key down and at the same time press the B key. The highlighted text is now also displayed in bold.

10 Finally we'll practise dragging with the mouse. First highlight the word 'world'. Now click once with the left mouse button on the highlighted word, and hold the mouse button down. Slowly move the mouse to the left. A small box attached to the mouse pointer shows that an object (in this case your word) is 'sticking' to the mouse pointer. When you have moved the mouse pointer in front of 'Welcome' release the left mouse button.

87

Congratulations! You have got through your workshop. If you had **problems** with one or two of the steps you should repeat the exercise or familiarise yourself with the mouse and keyboard functions using your own text. To work successfully with the PC it is essential that you can use the **basic functions** easily.

The joystick

We have almost reached the end of this chapter. But before closing we'll take a brief look at how a **joystick** works.

The position of the joystick – a loosely fixed lever – is registered by the computer. The joystick is attached to the computer's **game port** and is used by games that support a joystick. A driver program is not needed.

Joysticks are so called after aircraft control sticks and allow simulations to be controlled realistically and characters to be moved about the screen.

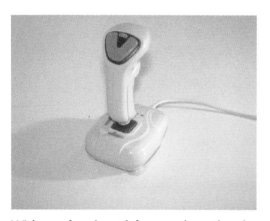

With **digital joysticks** each position is indicated as active or not active. Movements are possible in all directions, but not to intermediate stages. Digital joysticks are, however, particularly good value for money as simple switches are sufficient for working the control stick.

With **analog joysticks**, on the other hand, the position of the lever is determined through variable resistance. Analog joysticks are, therefore, recommended for realistic simulations, but are more expensive than digital models.

Quick progress check

Main topics: input devices and interfaces

You will come across five progress checks in this book. From the questions you can find out how much you have learned and whether there are any gaps in your knowledge.

If you have enough time to study this book you should write down your answers to the questions and compare them with the ones in the appendix.

➡ **Which standard does a PC keyboard comply with?**

_____

➡ **What is a codepage, and why is it useful?**

_____

_____

➡ **What do the following keys do?**

a) `Ctrl` _____

b) `Alt` _____

c) `Esc` _____

d) `Insert` _____

e) `Home`

f) `End`

g) `Print`

h) Function keys

➡ **How does a joystick differ from a mouse?**
How are these important input devices constructed?

➡ **What is a mouse driver, and why must one be installed before the mouse can be used?**

Which interface is the mouse normally connected to?

Which four interfaces are integrated in the PC as standard?

How does serial communication differ from parallel communication?
What advantages does the parallel interface have over the serial interface?

What is the purpose of the game interface?

91

Digital documents

What's in this chapter?

This chapter shows you how your PC manages and digitally stores data. We explain how floppy disk and hard disk drives work and the difference between magnetic and optical storage media.

You will then be able to use folders, drives and documents and create your own order structure for data storage. You will create and save your own text document, put it into folders, rename it and delete it. In this way you will learn the basic operations of your computer and how to use it.

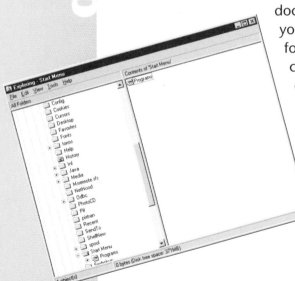

Your already know:

Your are going to learn about:

Mini-magnets instead of paper

In 1980 the media were talking about a **digital revolution** as the age of the personal computer was announced.

The **paperless office** was even prophesied because the computer would make paper records unnecessary. Seventeen years later you know that these futuristic forecasts have not come true. Even in state-of-the-art offices letters are sent on normal paper.

Even computer protagonists have come to doubt that the flood of paper has been stemmed. Hasn't the computer actually led to an avalanche of paper, from countless test printouts to printing electronically stored information for checking? Anyway, that's how it looks.

Paper-supported communication has at least become more professional and efficient. With **standard letter routines**, which are integral to most word-processing software, writing (completely personalised!) letters to several people has become very easy. Printouts from today's laser and ink jet printers are needle-sharp and meet even visual standards.

Furthermore data management and word-processing **software** has become much more user-friendly. You almost needed a degree in computer science to be able to use the first of these programs which was available for the IBM PC in 1980. The Windows revolution, on the other hand, allows them to be **used** almost **intuitively**, with no technical knowledge required from the user.

The futurologists Brad Wieners and David Pescovitz consider it improbable that the paperless office will become a reality in the foreseeable future. But, attempts are being made and sometimes solutions found, such as closing a contract over the Internet. In future you may be signing your contracts with the electronic equivalent of your signature, the **digital signature**

In this chapter we tell you what 'magnets' have to do with 'paper'. We show you how you put your own documents on a disk and how your PC's order system is set up.

Magnetic media store information

The way in which your PC stores data is not as revolutionary as it may appear at first. If you have ever recorded anything on a normal audio-cassette you already know how your PC stores information: magnetic particles are aligned in a magnetic field and so become 'intelligent'. Data storage media contain a very large number of these **magnetisable particles** and can store information accordingly.

Data storage media are devices that can store information and make it available again when requested.

So a magnet is supposed to be able to store data? Think back to the introductory chapter of this book where we explained the difference between analog signals and digital signals.

This is the most fundamental difference between the audio cassette and a **computer disk**. Whereas cassettes record sounds in the form of analog signals, disks store information as binary signals.

A magnetic particle corresponds to the state '1', a non-magnetic particle to '0'. The particles are firmly applied to a **platter** or **tape** and given a protective coating.

Permanent and temporary memory

Permanent memory holds digital information even when the power supply is removed.

Because magnetically stored information remains even when the power supply is removed, we talk about a **permanent memory**. When you switch off your PC, information stored on magnetic media remains. If you want to go back to the data at a later date the information can be loaded from the disk.

Think back to the procedures that occur when you **start up the PC**. The PC's **memory components** have to read data from a permanent memory, the **ROM**. If the power supply to the PC's memory component is removed the information contained in it is **erased** immediately. This is called a temporary memory and is based on electric memory principles that are not permanent.

The name 'permanent memory' is, however, deceptive in a way. The mini-magnets are **very sensitive** to magnetic interference. If you run a magnet over a previously non-magnetic particle the information '0' is converted into a '1', with the result that the stored information is now **incorrect**.

Read/Write head

A highly-developed and miniaturised **electromagnet** travels over the disk platter. When information is written there is always voltage on the magnet if the state '1' is to be written; on the other hand, the magnet is de-energised if a '0' state particle is to be assigned.

The process is the reverse when **reading** stored information. When the electromagnet goes over a magnetised spot a voltage is produced and so interpreted as '1'. Otherwise the head remains de-energised; this causes this state to be recognised as '0'.

The magnet is attached to an **arm** and can be moved over the disk platter. The mini-magnet is called the **read/write head** because data can be both loaded and stored with it.

Tapes and disks

The first of these magnetic media were very similar to audio-cassettes. In fact normal audio-cassettes could be used in the first of these storage devices. More advanced devices worked with their **own formats** and used tapes which were physically larger and had **more capacity**. The drives in which magnetic tapes can be written are called **streamers**.

Streamers are drives which can read and write magnetic tapes.

You still occasionally come across these magnetic tapes today. They are used primarily for creating backups. In practice, however, magnetic tapes do suffer from a number of **drawbacks** which have resulted in other types of data storage being preferred.

In **professional data systems technology**, on the other hand, magnetic tapes are still used today. A high-output magnetic tape can have a capacity of **48 gigabytes** and so can store about 2 million (!) full A4 pages of text.

Picture a magnetic tape in your mind. A sequence of magnetised and non-magnetised particles has been put on the tape. If information at the end of the tape is required, the magnetic tape has to be **rewound** – a **time-consuming process**. The so-called **access time** is very high compared with other storage media.

Access time describes the average period of time between accessing two different pieces of information.

Another disadvantage lies in the fact that **special software** has to be used. If, for example, you want to save a letter you created on your computer on a magnetic tape this can only be done indirectly via a driver.

Hard disks consist of read/write heads and magnetically coated platters that can store data.

The best alternatives are hard disks, the construction of which we have already described to you in principle: the magnetic particles are no longer put onto a tape, but onto a rotating disk instead.

The read/write head is attached to an arm which moves two-dimensionally over the disk platter. By the platter **rapidly rotating**, certain parts of the magnetic platter can be started at random.

There is, therefore, no time-consuming spooling, so the **access time of a hard disk** is much lower than that of magnetic tapes. Another advantage is in the construction of the hard disk. The read/write head does not come down on the surface of the

magnetic layer, as it does on magnetic tapes, but hovers over it **without making contact**.

The rapid rotation causes a **cushion of air** to form between the surface of the magnetic platter and the read/write head. This cushion carries the read/write head. Hard disks are thus **free from wear and tear** and have a **much longer life** than magnetic tapes.

During a dreaded **head crash** impurities get into the hard disk housing and destroy data.

The cushion of air is extremely narrow, much thinner than, for example, a speck of dust or the diameter of a human hair. If the slightest impurity gets into the casing of the magnetic platter the read/write head drags on the disk surface now and again and **in the process destroys all the data**. This very rare, but all the more dreaded event is called a **head crash** and destroys a large part of the data on a hard disk.

Modern hard disks are physically comparable with the **human palm** and contain up to 10 Gbytes (gigabytes) of data; that is about 420,000 A4 pages of text!

The following exercise shows you how to obtain information about your system's hard disk. If you work with Windows 95 or Windows NT you can work through the instructions step-by-step.

1 Start up your computer, and wait until Windows 95 or Windows NT 4.0 starts.

My Computer

2 Double-click the *My Computer* icon, which you will find in the top left-hand corner of the screen.

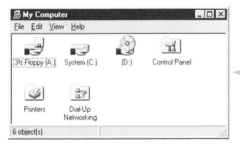

3 All the local disks are listed and represented by an icon in the window that appears.

System (C:)

4 Drive C: is always your first local hard disk. Hard disks are indicated with special icons. If your computer has more than one hard disk these are also listed.

5 Move the mouse pointer onto the icon, and press the right mouse button. Select Properties at the bottom of the context menu that appears.

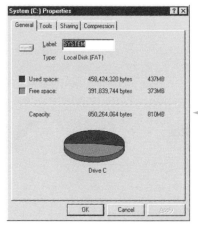

6 The window contains important data about your hard disk. The *Label* box displays the name of the disk, and a pie chart shows the space on this hard disk that is currently in use. So you can see at a glance whether there is sufficient capacity available.

Floppy disks

Floppy disks are very similar to hard disks. If you have a floppy disk to spare you should open it and have a close look inside it. The shiny greyish black surface contains the magnetic material and is **flexible**. This flexibility gave the **floppy disk** its name.

The read/write head, with which information can be read from the disk and written to it, is located in the **floppy disk drive**.

Floppy disks are **physically considerably more robust** than hard disks, but can store only a **fraction of the amount of data**.
  The read/write head comes down directly onto the magnetic surface when reading and writing. This **reduces the life** of a floppy disk significantly, and furthermore, friction causes **wear** to the disk and produces a grey dust which settles in the drive housing. If errors occur frequently when reading disks, special **cleaning disks** can be used.

For a long time floppy disks were available in two **sizes**: the older and now aged 5$^1/_4$" format stored 1.2 Mb (megabytes) of data, while the physically more sturdy 3$^1/_2$" format stores 1.44 Mb. Occasionally disks that can store 2.88 Mb are available.

When you compare the capacity of a floppy disk with that of hard disks, you will see the **most obvious drawback** of floppy disks. They can only hold a hundredth or even a thousandth of the amount of data that a hard disk can and in addition are comparatively slow.

Because of their small size, floppy disks are mainly used today for sending data, and to a lesser extent for creating **backups** of important data. Original software that you buy from a dealer is also supplied on **sets of floppy disks**. Toda, floppy disks are being replaced increasingly by modern types of media such as CD-ROMs, which we shall introduce you to later.

101

To ensure that data stored on floppy disks remains intact for a long time and sudden data losses are the exception, always follow these rules when handling floppy disks:

1 Never expose floppy disks to magnetic or electric fields.

2 Store floppy disks at room temperature. Intense heat or cold impairs the integrity of the data.

3 Never bend floppy disks, and do not place heavy objects on them.

4 Remove floppy disks from the drive after they have been written or read. This protects the read/write head.

Formatting

New floppy disks and hard disks consist of platters which are coated with a magnetic surface.

So that information stored later can be accessed in an orderly way, the surface must be provided with a **structure**. The magnetic particles are then grouped together in **precisely addressable segments**.

You can imagine this structure as being like a **sliced cake**. The individual slices are small units whose surfaces are formed from magnetic particles. This structure is obtained by **formatting**.

During **formatting** a standard structure is marked on a magnetisable surface. This is necessary for storing and reading information.

During the formatting of a floppy disk or hard disk any **data** on it is **lost**. Whereas in the past floppy disks always had to be formatted by the user before they could be used, today you normally find **factory-formatted floppy disks** in the shops.

In the following exercise you can work through the formatting of a floppy disk. Here, we use Windows 95; if you work with this operating system you can follow the steps for real.

For the example you will need either a new 3½″ floppy disk or one that you have finished with. During the formatting of a disk all the data on it is deleted irretrievably!

103

1 Start up your computer and wait until Windows 95 is loaded.

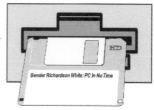

2 Put a 3½" disk in your floppy disk drive, metal shutter end first and labelled side upwards. You will feel a slight mechanical resistance.

My Computer

3 Double-click the *My Computer* icon, which you will find in the top left-hand corner of the desktop.

The *3¹/₂" Floppy (A:)* icon represents your floppy disk drive. Move the mouse pointer to the icon, and press the right mouse button. Select Format . . . in the context menu.

Click on the word *Full*, and then click *Start*.

105

6 Formatting now starts; you can follow its progress in the open window.

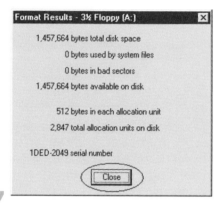

Format Results - 3½ Floppy (A:)

1,457,664 bytes total disk space

0 bytes used by system files

0 bytes in bad sectors

1,457,664 bytes available on disk

512 bytes in each allocation unit

2,847 total allocation units on disk

1DED-2049 serial number

Close

7 An information window confirms that formatting is complete. Click *Close*.

8 After formatting, double-click the 3$^{1}/_{2}$" *Floppy (A:)* icon. Another window, which shows you the contents of your floppy disk, is opened. Because the disk has just been formatted the window is empty.

During the formatting process you may have noticed an option field labelled **Quick**. You can activate this function if you want to reformat a preformatted floppy disk, for example, to delete the data contained on it.

Format type
- ⦿ Quick (erase)
- ○ Full
- ○ Copy system files only

Optical competition: CD-ROM & Co.

For a long time magnetic media were not only the ultimate in information storage, but also the only available technology. However, for some time now competition has been getting nearer: **optical media** are overtaking magnetic storage devices.

Modern data stores make use of the **ability of light** to be **reflected** by flat surfaces. You know about the developments in the audio field where innovations always seem to precede corresponding ones in the computer field.

Just as the audio-cassette is being superseded by the compact disc (CD), conventional floppy disks will certainly die out in the foreseeable future. The 'magic disk', the **CD-ROM** (short for 'Compact Disc Read Only Memory'), has really revolutionised digital storage technology.

Unlike hard disks and floppy disks, the **CD-ROM** is a storage medium which works on optical principles.

We list the most important advantages of the CD-ROM below. Then we describe how data is stored on the silver disk.

107

Data integrity

This is a significant advantage over magnetic media. Whereas hard disks and floppy disks are very sensitive to magnetic influences and so must be handled carefully, CD-ROMs are **more robust** in this respect. **Scratches** on the surface of the silver disk can certainly lead to **data loss**, but still handling and above all storing them is more straightforward.

Capacity

Whereas in the past, promotional programs, electronic catalogues and driver software in particular were supplied on floppy disks, this data now nearly always comes on CD-ROMs, which hold up to 600 Mb. The trend towards **multimedia presentations** supports the optical medium as there is not enough space on a floppy disk for the graphics, video and audio data.

Price

The cheapness of CD-ROMs makes it possible to produce even small runs viably. If you worked out a capacity/price quotient, no other media would bear comparison. The extremely attractive price of CD-ROM drives means that all those who want to can use CD-ROM technology.

However, two drawbacks are characteristic of CD-ROM technology and make it **impossible** to use the silver disk for **some purposes**. For one thing modern CD-ROM drives are clearly **inferior** to even the slowest hard disks when it comes to **speed**. The clearest disadvantage, however, is revealed in the name: data can certainly be read, but it can only be put on the CD-ROM with special, expensive devices, called **CD-ROM burners**. If CD-ROMs are to be used for data backup purposes a CD-ROM burner is required.

WHAT'S THIS?

Normal CD-ROM drives can only read CD-ROMs. A **CD-ROM burner** is required to write data.

When handling CD-ROMs follow the advice below.

1 Never expose CD-ROMs to direct sunlight. It can cause the plastic disk to warp and become unusable.

2 Never touch the surface with your fingers. Traces of grease and sweat that are left behind cause problems when reading the data.

3 Store the silver disks in the plastic covers supplied. Dust will not get on the surface then.

4 Label the upper side of the CD-ROM with a soft felt-tip pen only.

How to read and write optical media

Because there are no magnetisable particles a medium that operates optically cannot work with voltages, which are produced by a magnetic field.

In the case of optical media, **miniature mirrors** take on the role of the magnetic particles. If a directed light beam hits one of these mirrors it is reflected. Such a reflection can be picked up with a device similar to a **light barrier** and interpreted as '1'. In contrast with this there are small **indentations** on the surface of the silver CD-ROM called **pits**. If a light beam hits one of these pits it is 'swallowed' and the lack of a signal is interpreted as '0'. Now you can see why a **fingerprint** can lead to **data chaos**: if the laser beam hits a dirty spot it may not be reflected any more and be wrongly be interpreted as '0'.

In order to put as much information as possible in a given area the diameter of the light beam must be as small as possible, that is to say, it must be **focused**. In practice a laser beam is used which scans the surface of the CD-ROM. The laser beam works with a very **low intensity** and so does not damage the surface. As the scanning process is contact-free the CD drives are **not subject to physical interference**.

Writing data on the CD-ROM involves making the indentations. Because this requires more energy from the laser beam the afore-mentioned CD-ROM burner, which burns pits on to the surface, is used.

Incidentally, CD-ROMs do **not not need formatting**. This completely different type of data storage does not require a standard structure to be applied as is the case with magnetic media.

Carrying out minor repairs yourself

Don't worry – we are not going to ask you to get a screwdriver and unscrew the hard disk or other hardware.

However, you can fix **minor problems** on your floppy disks or the hard disk yourself. Windows 95 and Windows NT 4.0 as well as most other operating systems have **help programs** as standard, which automatically check disks for errors and immediately repair minor faults.

It may be that when data is frequently written and read, an application program does not close a document properly. This leaves its mark on the hard disk and produces **junk files**. These errors are called **logical faults** because the mechanics or electronics of the hard disk itself have not been damaged, only the file structure.

A **repair program** detects these faulty structures and corrects them. You should use the maintenance programs at regular intervals to prevent unintentional chaos on your hard disk. You should run the software every two to four weeks because, as the saying goes, **better safe than sorry**.

Incidentally, you can save yourself the trouble if you have installed the **Microsoft Plus** package. The Plus Software 'remembers' when your hard disk was last checked and regularly runs the necessary check in the background. It's a shame that the basic version of Windows 95 doesn't have this practical feature!

The following exercise shows how, using Windows 95, you can carry out minor repairs with the **ScanDisk** program.

1 Start up your computer, and wait until Windows 95 is loaded.

My Computer

2 Double-click the *My Computer* icon.

111

3 Move the mouse pointer to the icon of the disk you want to check, and press the right mouse button. In the context menu select Properties by clicking on it with the left mouse button.

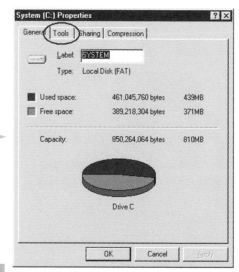

4 We have already shown you the window which appears. Activate the index card *Tools*.

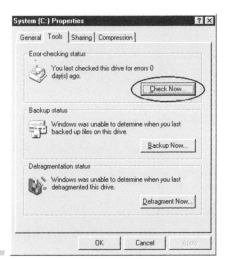

5 In the upper part of the window you will see the heading 'Error-checking'. Confirm this function by clicking *Check Now* . . .

6 Confirm the next dialog box without changing the settings.

113

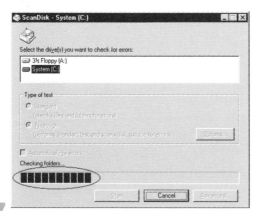

7 The hard disk or floppy disk is now checked. During checking a progress indicator allows you to monitor the areas that have been checked.

8 After the check you receive a list of all the errors found and are told whether they were able to be fixed.

Tidying up using Disk defragmenter

From time to time everyone has to tidy up their desk or go through their files. If you do not sort out your documents every now and again **chaos** will become a part of everyday life. Invoices 'disappear' under a pile of junk mail, and who is going to look through there?

The situation is the same with your computer. You create text documents with your word-processing program and save them on the hard disk. When you want to access the digital letter again some time later the **search** begins and soon develops into a time-consuming and frustrating activity.

Your computer relieves you of a large part of the routine tidying up work. Pieces of files ('fragments') are **strung together in an orderly way** and so become **sorted**. Your PC can then access data much **more quickly** because it can save itself search operations: instead of searching for pieces of a file and picking out the individual pieces it can take the sorted fragments as a whole.

This principle can also be transferred to your office. If you store all the documents for a project in different folders and are asked to find all the individual papers it is time-consuming. If you have, however, filed all related papers in **one folder** you will be able to find the information much more quickly.

The sorting of data on your hard disk happens very much more quickly. Smaller hard disks are **tidied in around ten minutes**, larger ones need about thirty minutes – depending of course on the state of the hard disk.

If you get the impression that accessing information is taking much **longer than it used to** it is high time you tidied up your hard disk. In order to keep things tidy and prevent data chaos you should sort your hard disk about **once a month**, more often if is used frequently.

If you come across an external program that promises to tidy up the hard disk you must make sure it is 'Windows 95-compatible'. Other software can destroy the data on your hard disk.

The following exercise shows you how, using Windows 95, to tidy up your hard disk with the **disk defragmenter** system program. Disk defragmenter was installed on your PC when the operating system was installed and so is available as standard.

115

1 In *My Computer* click with the right mouse button on the icon of the hard disk you want to tidy.

In the context menu select Properties by clicking with the left mouse button.

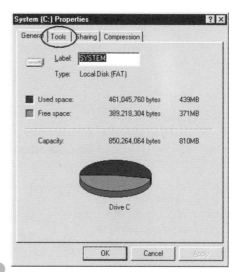

2 You are familiar with the dialog box which now appears. Activate the index card *Tools*.

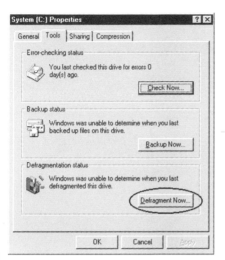

3 Select the defragmentation routine by clicking 'Defragment Now' in the *Defragmentation* box. You will be told how long it is since the last defragmentation.

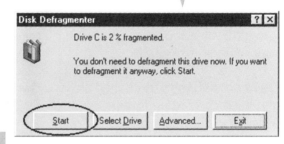

4 The following window displays the degree of fragmentation as a percentage. Click *Start*.

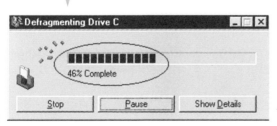

5 The defragmentation process is displayed by a progress bar.

117

Data structure: drawers in the computer

The next few pages in this chapter show you how the information on your disks is organised.

In the section about hard disks showed we reckoned approximately **420,000 A4** pages can be stored on a 10 Gb hard disk. If your home or office PC has 2 Gb that is still 84,000 pages of text. You can imagine that such an unbelievably large amount of data requires **efficient** and well **thought-out structuring**.

Before we describe your PC's filing system, let us analyse the **order system** in your office. Fortunately the developers of PC disks have **used real life as a basis** so the logic will be familiar to you.

Your office	Your computer
You work at a **desk** which forms the 'headquarters' of your work so to speak	The **desktop** of your PC corresponds to the desk; it also has central functions
There are **cabinets** in your office which contain folders	**Data storage media** (a hard disk, for example) also contain folders
Folders, which – grouped under subject matter – contain separate papers, are stored in the cabinets	Data storage media also contain **folders** which can hold documents in digital form
Separate **documents** constitute the smallest unit in the office	**Electronic documents** are also the smallest storable units
Files that are thrown in the bin are no longer required	The **Windows Recycle Bin** fulfils the same purpose; files deposited in it are deleted

The next few pages show you examples of how you can use and operate the separate structures.

The desktop: virtual desk

Very few users realise that the visible interface that appears immediately after the start of Windows 95 corresponds to the 'desktop'.

The Windows concept describes the desktop as the **central co-ordination point** of your activities. In fact the similarity between the Windows desktop and your desk is unmistakable.

The **desktop** is the central interface of your PC and corresponds to a desk.

You can imagine the individual icons that appear after the start as being **objects** (items) that you have put on your desk. These items may be application programs such as 'Word for Windows' or a favourite document.

You can, therefore, **put any data** on the desktop. If, for example, you often access data from the floppy disk drive the drive can be put on the desktop. The following exercise shows how to move an icon to the desktop.

1 Switch on your computer and wait until Windows 95 or Windows NT 4.0 is loaded. Double-click the *My Computer* icon.

119

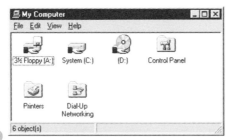

2 A window appears which contains icons of your drives.

3 Click with the left mouse button on the *3¹/₂" Floppy (A:)* icon, and hold the left button down. The floppy disk icon is now 'sticking' to the mouse pointer and can be moved.

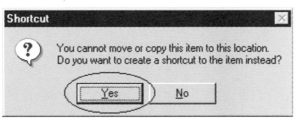

Shortcut ☒

❓ You cannot move or copy this item to this location. Do you want to create a shortcut to the item instead?

[<u>Y</u>es]   <u>N</u>o

4 Drag the icon to any free space on the visible desktop, and release the left button. Confirm the message by clicking *Yes*.

Shortcut to 3½
Floppy (A)

5 The new icon is put
on the desktop and is
called *3¹/₂" Floppy (A:)*.

6 Then check
that the icon works
correctly. Place any
floppy disk (perhaps one containing
data) in drive A:, and double-click
the newly created icon. The contents
of the floppy disk are displayed.

In this way you can put any item on the virtual desk. If you want to
practise moving one again you can drag your system hard disk or
the CD-ROM drive to the desktop.

In the fifth step above you confirmed a message saying that a
shortcut would be created; your new icon was correspondingly
called 'Shortcut to . . . '.

A **shortcut** is a
reference to
the original
icon.

When you, therefore, click the 'Shortcut to . . . '
icon this corresponds to a click on the floppy
disk icon in the 'My Computer' window.
This doesn't change even if you rename the
shortcut icon.

The Recycle Bin

You will certainly have noticed the **Recycle Bin**. You can deposit items you no longer want in it and so **delete** them. Just as with a normal bin, if you 'throw' a file in the Recycle Bin by mistake you can undo the deletion. It is only when the Recycle Bin is emptied that all the files in it are **deleted for good**.

The following example shows you how to use the Recycle Bin. Here, we are using Windows 95 or Windows NT 4.0; however, you will also find a corresponding function under OS/2 and graphical Unix interfaces.

The shortcut we created earlier is to be moved into the Recycle Bin in the following example.

1 Click the *Shortcut to 3¹/₂" Floppy (A:)* icon you have just created with the left mouse button, and hold the button down.

Shortcut to 3½ Floppy (A)

Recycle Bin

2 While holding down the left button move the mouse to the Recycle Bin icon. The shortcut icon is attached to the mouse pointer. Then release the mouse button.

Recycle Bin

3 The shortcut has disappeared from the desktop. You will now see some crumpled paper in the Recycle Bin icon: a visual indication that it contains one or more files.

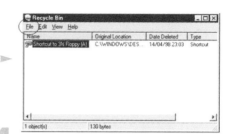

4 Now double-click the Recycle Bin icon; the top item is *Shortcut to . . .*. Open the File menu, and select Restore. The deleted file is restored and the associated icon put on the desktop.

5 Throw the shortcut in the Recycle Bin again, and click the Recycle Bin with the right button. Now select EMPTY RECYCLE BIN in the context menu that appears.

123

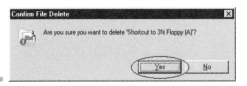

6 A warning message points out that the documents in the Recycle Bin will be deleted for good. Confirm the message.

Recycle Bin

7 The Recycle Bin icon has been changed slightly: an empty bin indicates that there is no longer any data stored in it.

TIP: Files are not only put in the Recycle Bin when you drag their icon to the Recycle Bin icon. Even when you select the delete function of user software, files are first thrown in the Recycle Bin.

A word of caution at this point. There are dangers in using the Recycle Bin. Take the following case:

An employee in an engineering office works with **sensitive** and **secret** documents which contain the design plans for a scientific measuring device. He works on his PC during the day, saves the secret documents on a floppy disk which he locks in the company's safe. He deletes the original documents from the hard disk of his PC using the Recycle Bin function.

But it could happen that an industrial spy takes the opportunity to restore the data from the Recycle Bin and give it to competitors.

So, if you work with sensitive information empty the Recycle Bin regularly!

File manager

There are plenty of software packages for **managing data structure**. Every manufacturer of a graphical operating system provides its products with a **file manager**.

A **file manager** manages a computer's data centrally and is supplied with all graphical operating systems.

Windows Explorer is a stand-alone program that allows data to be manipulated. It is completely independent of the Windows 95 desktop and should not be confused with this.

The Windows 3 file manager was actually called 'File Manager'. In Windows 95 and Windows NT 4.0 this has given way to the considerably more powerful and user-friendly 'Windows Explorer'.

In the following example we briefly show you how to use Windows Explorer, which in a way is representative of numerous other file managers. More about handling files and folders will be explained later. If you work with Windows 95 or Windows NT 4.0 you can apply the example directly.

1 Click the Start button in the bottom left-hand corner of the Windows 95 or Windows NT 4.0 screen with the right mouse button. Select Explore in the following context menu.

2 Click the top item *Desktop* in the left-hand part of the Exploring window *(All Folders)*. If the item is not visible you can use the scroll bar at the right-hand edge of the window.

3 You will see a hierarchy of different levels. The highest level constitutes the *desktop*; the associated icon shows a desk.

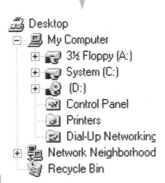

4 The second level includes the items that are currently on the desktop. You will see *My Computer* among them as well as the *Recycle Bin* towards the bottom.

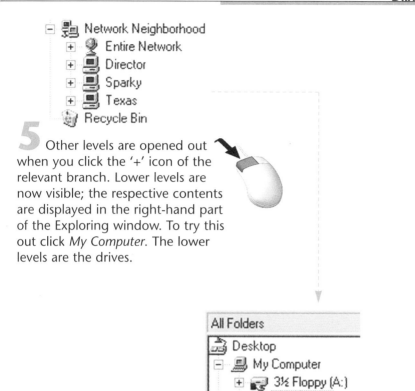

5 Other levels are opened out when you click the '+' icon of the relevant branch. Lower levels are now visible; the respective contents are displayed in the right-hand part of the Exploring window. To try this out click *My Computer*. The lower levels are the drives.

6 You can close the levels at any time by clicking the '-' icon. Leave the *My Computer* level by clicking the minus sign in front of it. The drive icons, which had opened out, disappear.

Drive labels

Up until now you have taken it for granted that the drives are given a letter and end with a **colon**.

Do you remember when we created the shortcut to the floppy disk drive together in the earlier workshop? The label that you looked for in 'My Computer' was '3$^1/_2$ Floppy (**A:**)'; likewise the hard disk is assigned the identifier **C:**.

127

The CD-ROM drive and all the other data storage devices you find in 'My Computer' also have a **letter**. This so-called **drive letter** clearly identifies a data storage device on your system. The letter is always followed by a **colon**.

Each of your computer's drives is given a **drive letter** via which data can be read and written. A letter may, therefore, only be used once in a computer system.

If, for example, you copy a file from a floppy disk to the hard disk using the mouse and drag the file to the hard disk icon, the corresponding computer instruction in the 'computer language' could read: 'Copy file X from drive A: to drive C:'.

This convention is **very common** and not only applies to Windows 95. It stems from the early days of computers when drives were also actuated with a drive letter.

Some computer systems are an exception to the rule and work with a completely different syntax. These are, however, special systems which you will not normally have to deal with.

The letters A: and B: are reserved for **floppy disk drives** so that you can run a **maximum of two floppy disk drives** in one computer. Your PC is probably only equipped with one drive so that the identifier B: is not used.

The other letters can be assigned variably. C: usually indicates your **local hard disk**; if you have two or more hard disks or if your only hard disk is partitioned, the identifiers D:, E:, etc., are used.

Your **CD-ROM drive** is usually given the next free identifier after the labels for the floppy disk and hard disk drives have been assigned.

If your computer is part of a network other letters can be assigned so that you may actuate **up to 26 drives** (corresponding to the letters of the alphabet) on your computer.

Folders archive files

My Computer is a folder, albeit a special one. Your computer's disks and printer are concealed in this folder.

You already, therefore, know how you have to 'operate' a folder. A **double-click** on the folder icon **opens** the folder. It is closed when you **close** the **window**.

In older literature in particular, folders are often described as 'directories'. DOS versions also use 'directories'. But when Microsoft revolutionised the computer world with its Windows 95 it coined the term 'folder'.

You can set up as many folders as you like on your hard disk. The great advantage lies in the possibility of setting up **subfolders** in **several hierarchies** as the basis for a useful structure.

You can thus set up **very flexible** folders. We will introduce you to two typical folder structures so that you can establish a folder system to meet your individual needs.

1st example

Make sure you give the folders names which are as unambiguous as possible and relate to their contents, in order to avoid later misunderstandings particularly in more complex folder structures!

The two main folders in the first example are called **Work Files** and **Personal Files,** which aptly describes their contents.

Let's look at the other folders that have been set up in the main folder 'Work Files'. The first-level folders are called **Incoming invoices, Outgoing invoices, Outstanding items** and **Other correspondence**.

Other folders, which overall form the third level, have been set up within these folders. In the folder **Incoming invoices**, for example, there are four subfolders – **Invoices I-98** to **Invoices IV-98**.

129

Later documents can be filed in these folders, and quickly found again when required. For example, an employee looking for an outgoing invoice from the second quarter intuitively accesses the folder **Work Files/Outgoing invoices/Invoices II-98**.

2nd example

In the second example customer data is not sorted according to correspondence category, but according to the customer's name. The main folder, for example, is called **Work Files**; the folders of the second hierarchical level are called **Johnson, Harris** and **Smith**. Finally, the folders corresponding to categories are at the third level, for instance **Invoices, Quotations** and **Other Business**.

Labelling folders

Folder names can have **up to 256 characters**. You can use special characters, such as the hyphen; some characters including the full-stop and the colon are reserved for the operating system and so you cannot use them.

The optimum name contains a **maximum of 15 characters** and describes the folder as aptly as possible. Instead of 'Invoices 3' you should call your folder 'Invoices May-July'.

The following exercise shows you how to create, rename and delete folders up to the third level. If you work with Windows 95 or Windows NT 4.0 you can follow the steps for real.

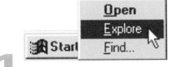

1 Click the Start button with the right mouse button, and select Explore in the context menu.

2 Open the folder *My Computer* by clicking the '+' sign in front of it.

3 Select your local hard disk by clicking *Hard disk C:* once. The item is now highlighted in blue, and all existing folders are displayed in the right-hand part of the screen.

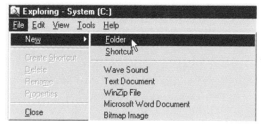

4 First of all we are going to create a new main folder and call it *Work Files*. Click File in the menu bar, and point to New.

131

Contents of 'System (C:)'

New Folder

5 Click Folder at the top to create a new folder. A new folder icon with the name *New Folder* immediately appears on the right-hand side of the screen. Confirm the name by pressing the ⬅ key.

Contents of 'System (C:)'

New Fc...

| Explore |
| Open |
| Find... |
| Add to Zip |
| Add to New Folder.zip |
| Sharing... |
| Send To ▶ |
| Cut |
| Copy |
| Create Shortcut |
| Delete |
| Rename |
| Properties |

6 Next the new folder is to be renamed. Click on the newly created folder with the right mouse button, and select Rename in the context menu. Type *Work Files* as the new folder name, and confirm this with *OK*.

Contents of 'System (C:)'

☐ Work Files

7 The folder *Work Files* now appears on the left-hand side of the Exploring screen.

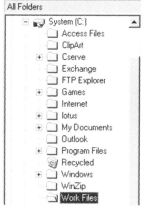

8 To create other subfolders you must first select the hierarchically higher folder. So click the folder *Work Files* with the left mouse button.

☐ Work Files
　　☐ Incoming invoices

9 Select File/New/Folder again, and create a folder called *Incoming invoices*. If you then click on the folder *Work Files* the folder *Incoming invoices* should be displayed on the right-hand side of the window as the contents of the main folder.

133

⊟ ☐ Work Files
   ⊟ ☐ Incoming invoices
       ☐ Urgent

10 For practice create a third subfolder, which should be added below the folder *Incoming invoices* and given the name Urgent.

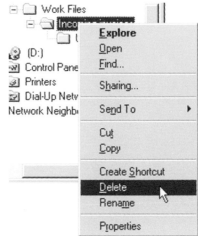

11 Finally, the *Incoming invoices* level and the subfolder *Urgent* it contains are to be deleted. Click the folder *Incoming invoices* with the right mouse button, and select Delete in the context menu.

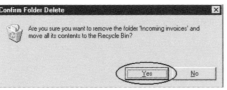

12 Confirm the warning message which indicates that the selected folder will be deleted together with its contents.

You now know the **basic operations** required for creating and manipulating folders. On this basis you should now create your own structure into which you can later incorporate your data.

You can rename folders more quickly by clicking the folder twice. However, you must leave more time between the two clicks than when double-clicking. The folder is then highlighted in blue as usual and can be renamed.

Files are documents

Whereas a folder is a container for files, so is useful only as an organisational tool, files themselves contain saved information.

A **file** can contain an **executable program**, such as the ScanDisk program we looked earlier in this chapter. Even Windows 95 stores internal operating system information as files. Files, therefore, form a **central base** for all information processing.

However, as far as you are concerned, files are electronic documents which were, for example, created by a word processor or graphics program and then put on disk.

Files are the **smallest units of data** that you will deal with.

Filenames

Early DOS and Windows versions could allocate names to files which were a maximum of eight characters long. However, in practice eight characters were not enough, as users soon found out. Even at that time, Unix, OS/2, Apple Macintosh and various other operating systems could work with considerably longer filenames.

The problem with the eight character restriction was that the file contents were often **not described**. Imagine you write several letters to Mr Johnson. The file can be given the following names:

JOHNSON1
LETTERJO
LTRJOHNS
LTJOHNS1

You will realise that these word combinations are not particularly meaningful and you will certainly be faced with a problem when you want to access the file again some time later. **What** did 'JOHNSON1' **contain**? What do you call the second letter to Mr Johnson? 'LETTERJ . . . ' has already been used. Furthermore no distinction is made between upper and lower case.

With Windows 95 and Windows NT the Windows world finally came of age in this respect. Filenames can now contain a **maximum of 256 characters**, so there is enough room for longer and descriptive filenames. The letter to Mr Johnson could, for example, be called:

'Letter to Mr Johnson, in which he is invited to the conference on 25.11.99'

The extended filename system also distinguishes **upper and lower case**. Some special characters including the **comma** and **hyphen** are also allowed.

Interestingly, Microsoft described this innovation, which is actually very convenient, as 'the innovation of the computer world'. However, Apple and manufacturers of other operating systems gave their users the facility to use long filenames much earlier.

If you use software under Windows 95 which was developed for earlier Windows versions, files and folders cannot be named using the new 256 character convention. In this case filenames can contain a maximum of eight characters.

File extensions

Even in the dark ages of the computer it was possible to extend the eight character filename by exactly **three additional characters**. For this reason this early system is known by the name **8+3**.

This so-called **file extension** indicates the **file type**. The three characters are conventionally separated from the filename by a dot. The letter to Mr Johnson, for example, could, therefore, be:

JOHNSON1.TXT

JOHNSON1.DOC

JOHNSON1.XYZ

You'd probably guess correctly that the extension **TXT** refers to **text** which is stored in the file. Application software uses this ending to establish whether the file can be read. So you will be able to process a text file with a word processor, but not with a graphics program.

The following table lists some typical file extensions and their meanings. In the appendix we have printed a comprehensive survey of the most important and most common file extensions.

File extension	Type
TXT	Text file
DOC	Special Word text file
GIF	Graphics file
XLS	Microsoft Excel spreadsheet
MDB	Microsoft Access database
HTML	Internet web page

The following steps show you how you can write your first file to your hard disk. As an example we first create a test text which is then stored in a new folder under a suitable name.

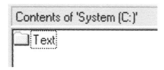

1 Using Windows Explorer create a main folder called *Text* on your hard disk C:. The test file will be stored in this folder later.

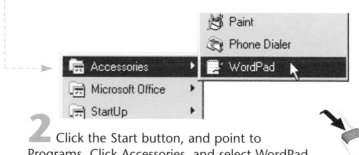

2 Click the Start button, and point to Programs. Click Accessories, and select WordPad.

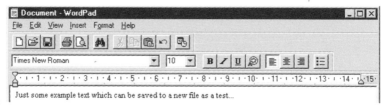

3 Now type a few lines of any text.

4 In the File menu select Save as . . . The *Save As* window appears and asks you to type a filename in the File name box. Click the suggestion *Document* with the mouse, and type 'My test file' as the name.

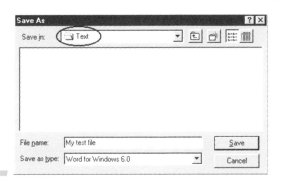

5 Now click *My Computer*, and select your local hard disk C:. There you will find the folder *Text* created in the first step. Open this by double-clicking it.

Contents of 'Text'

My test file

 **6** You can now write the file to the hard disk to the folder *Text* by clicking the *Save* button. The file should now be displayed as the contents of the folder *Text* in the right-hand part of the screen.

Wildcards

The filename system recognises **variables** (called **wildcards**) that you can use for file selections.

It sounds very complicated, but is used very often in practice. An example shows you what a **file selection** is and why it is so important.

If, for example, you saved a file called **REED**, but now cannot remember exactly how it was spelt you may have some work ahead of you to find it. After all as well as **REED** there is **REID, READ** and **READE**.

Wildcard '?'
(question mark)
replaces any
character in a
word or phrase.

Wildcard '*'
(asterisk)
replaces any
long string.

You can replace characters with wildcards. If, for example, you tell a search program to list all files with the name 'R??D' you will get a list that takes into account three of the four possible spellings. You will have guessed by now that the question mark replaces any letter. So the file selection 'R????' would list all five-letter filenames beginning with R.

The file system also recognises another variable, the '*'. The asterisk replaces any combination of characters. The selection 'R*', for example, would produce all filenames of any length beginning with 'R'.

Finding files

Most operating systems allow you to **search** for **files** on disks. This is important if you have worked with your computer for a while and vaguely remember having saved a particular file but can no longer remember which folder it is in.

Looking in the various folders is certainly not very convenient as well as being time-consuming. Instead let your PC look for you!

Early operating systems often required users to use a cryptic interface; modern systems, on the other hand, only ask you to **enter a search pattern**.

The following steps show you the search function integrated into Windows 95 and Windows NT 4.0 (which are representative of many other systems). We use the file 'My test file' created earlier as an example. It is to be tracked down using the search function.

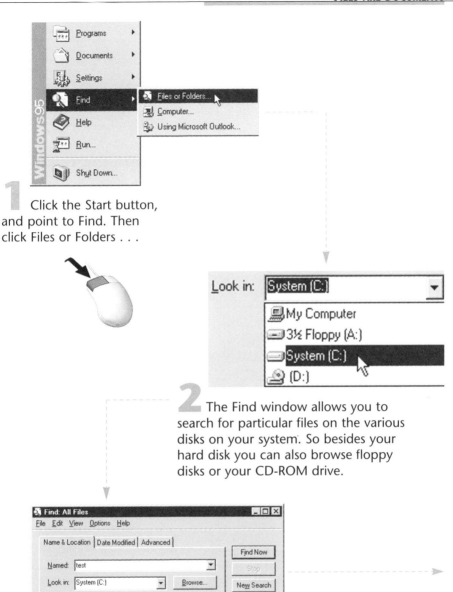

1 Click the Start button, and point to Find. Then click Files or Folders . . .

2 The Find window allows you to search for particular files on the various disks on your system. So besides your hard disk you can also browse floppy disks or your CD-ROM drive.

3 In the *Named* box type the search pattern 'test', a part of the filename 'My test file'.

141

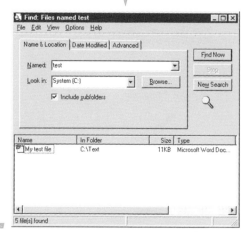

Click *Find Now*
to start the search.

Just a few seconds later your computer
indicates a find and displays it in the
bottom part of the Find window. The folder
in which the file is stored is also given.

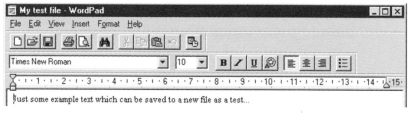

You can now have a close look
at the contents of the file by double-
clicking the find directly in the Find
window. The associated application
(in our example WordPad) is started
and the document loaded.

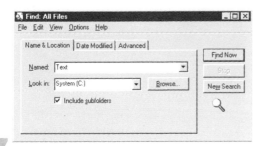

7 For practice you can find the folder *Text* by using a suitable search pattern.

Moving files

In your daily work you may want to move documents between folders. In Windows this **moving** procedure occurs by 'drag and drop'.

Drag and drop describes a convenient mouse-controlled procedure for moving items

A typical example of moving files is in a **storage system**. For instance, Invoices from the previous year can be moved to a storage folder so that your folder system is ready for the next year.

The following exercise shows you how to move the sample document in the 'Texts' folder (from the previous exercise) first to the desktop and then into another folder.

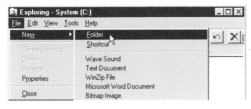

1 Create a new main folder on your hard disk C: and call it *Files 1999*.

143

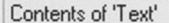

Contents of 'Text'

My test file

2 Open Windows Explorer, and display
the contents of the folder *Text*. It contains
the document 'My test file'.

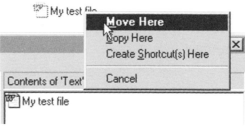

3 Click the file icon with the right mouse
button, and hold the button down. Drag the icon,
which is now attached to the mouse pointer, to
any free place on the desktop. If you now release
the mouse button a
context menu appears.
Click on Move Here.

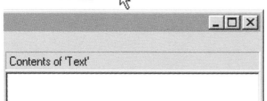

4 The icon which has been moved is now
stored on the desktop and deleted in the
original *Text* folder.

Contents of 'Files 1997'

My test file

5 Now click the newly created folder *Files 1997* in Windows Explorer. Drag the file icon to the folder in the same way. The icon disappears from the desktop and instead is stored in the folder.

You can move files directly without having to use the roundabout way of the desktop. To do this, a second Explorer window is opened and arranged next to the first one. Files or complete folders can then be moved between the windows.

Shortcut or copying?

One final, important tip for you at the end of this chapter to take with you through the file system jungle concerns the difference between **copying** and a **shortcut**.

The previous exercise gave you the opportunity of not only moving the item attached to the mouse pointer, but also creating a copy or a shortcut. Earlier in this chapter we explained what a shortcut is.

Whereas a shortcut only represents a **reference** to a file, whenever you select 'Create a copy' a second **copy** is produced which is **independent of the original**.

If you amend the original file the shortcut is adjusted accordingly. If you make several copies of one document and work with all of them, it can be confusing trying to remember which is the most up to date.

In general you should, therefore, **always** create **a shortcut** and only make copies in **exceptional cases**, for example as a backup in case you accidentally delete the original.

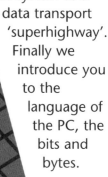

6

How your computer works

What's in
this chapter?

First of all we shall show you what tasks are too much for a computer and where a human is superior.

We explain what a processor is and the distinctions between processor generations. In addition we show you the connection between the clock rate and the speed and describe the function of the bus system as a data transport 'superhighway'. Finally we introduce you to the language of the PC, the bits and bytes.

Your already know:

Your are going to learn about:

147

Not really intelligent, but incredibly quick

Can you add up several million numbers in a second? Of course not, but, after all, that's what the computer is for. The 'electronic computing brain' seems to be a real multi-talent. It works out the square root of any number in a flash, finds logarithms, calculates the sine and tangent of angles and adds, subtracts, divides and multiplies in fractions of a second.

But is the computer really so superior to us, as it first appears to be? We have already explained that the computer has great difficulty in, for example, deciphering something as 'simple' as speech.

It also fails at many other things: no computer can decipher handwriting with great accuracy. Whereas you can often read a handwritten letter even if the sender has 'illegible' handwriting, a PC won't even get close, despite all its expensive electronics.

You may be familiar with the following sentences; if not try to make sense of them:

Time flies like an arrow. Fruit flies like a banana.

The words 'flies' and 'like' appear twice but with different functions. You may have had to read the sentence a couple of times before you really understood it. However, something like this gives a computer almost insoluble problems. Grammar checkers are certainly available, but are full of errors.

Translating complete texts from English into, say, German is also asking far too much of PCs. Really good software, e.g. the Langenscheidt Translator 'T1', certainly produces amazingly usable results, but it definitely needs a (human) proofreader.

The nub of the problem is this: the computer does not have the razor-sharp mind that differentiates the human from the electronic helper. When it comes to carrying out so-called 'constructive tasks' the computer is no match for a human.

WHAT'S THIS?

An **algorithm** or an **arithmetical** routine is a list of defined commands and arithmetical steps that are processed by a computer.

On the other hand, tasks which can be processed in accordance with an instruction can be dealt with much more quickly by the computer. It is for these 'receptive' tasks that computers are useful. This type of defined sequence for the operations to be carried out is called an 'algorithm' or 'arithmetical routine'.

Computer engineers have directed their efforts at providing computers with some intelligence of their own. The resulting discipline 'Artificial Intelligence' has generally achieved some amazing results, but is not really comparable with the neural intelligence of a human being.

You may have followed the big chess event in May 1997. The high-performance IBM computer 'Deep Blue' beat the world chess champion Kasparov. The Grand Master was checkmated in the final, deciding game after only ten minutes.

To outsiders this moment seemed to be the triumph of technology over humans. But in the end 'Deep Blue' had only processed an algorithm. It had worked out all the possible subsequent moves of the world chess champion incredibly quickly and picked the most likely one according to the 'rules' it had been programmed with.

Is it not more surprising that it takes an unbelievably powerful multimillion dollar computer to defy a human?

In this chapter we shall describe how a computer works and introduce you to the world of 'bits and bytes' which we have kept from you as much as possible so far.

149

The processor

The processor, which forms the core unit of every computer, is in a way like a brain adapted for a computer. You find this type of processor in numerous appliances, even in those where you would never have thought there would be a computer chip.

About 80% of processors are used in non-computer-related appliances, such as washing machines, lawnmowers, electric toothbrushes, televisions, stereo equipment, petrol pumps, etc.

The word 'computer' is after all derived from the verb 'to compute'. A processor can actually do nothing more than carry out all types of calculations incredibly quickly. The term often used for the processor is CPU.

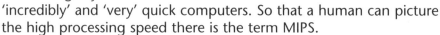

Up until now we have only written vaguely about 'incredibly' and 'very' quick computers. So that a human can picture the high processing speed there is the term MIPS.

The **CPU** (Central Processing Unit) is the core unit of every computer. It carries out calculations and co-ordinates the processes in the computer.

MIPS is the abbreviation for 'Millions of Instructions Per Second' and describes the processing speed of a computer.

The MIPS rating indicates how many individual addition and subtraction commands (instructions) a particular processor can carry out per second. Powerful computers can add or subtract up to 100 million numbers in just one second.

There is, however, a certain danger linked with the MIPS rating. It is wrong to consider it as the only measure of the total power of a computer, as the following example illustrates:

Wait states slow the computer down unnecessarily and so reduce its actual computing power.

If our 100 MIPS processor receives its data from slower components which do not deliver the data to be computed at a sufficient speed, the processor has to insert 'wait states' and so is slowed down. However, some technology avoids these wait states and so make the processes in the PC more efficient.

Different CPU generations

Distinctions are made between several processor generations according to their internal structure and design. In general a new processor generation means a significant increase in power which expands the computer's general capabilities.

Several PC generations have developed from the actual processor generations, as a new processor also required more powerful components that could supply data at a faster rate. So, in older generation PCs, you always find slower hard disks than in modern Pentium PCs which have high-performance hard disks with higher capacities and speeds.

151

The market leader in processors, Intel, has brought out processors at irregular intervals which represent the different generations. Other manufacturers' CPUs are always compatible with the corresponding Intel models.

The very first PC processor appeared in 1979. It was given the name XT, which stood for Extended Technology. Compared with modern processors its computing power was ridiculously low: a Pentium processor computes around 200 times faster!

The XT was followed three years later, in 1982, by its successor, the AT. This contraction stood for Advanced Technology. PCs with this new processor were priced out around £4000 and remained the preserve of professionals.

In 1986 Intel introduced the next generation, the 386 processor, and the 486 followed in 1989.

Modern PCs, probably yours included, have a Pentium processor. This grand-sounding name has a legal history. Because of the great success of this processor Intel's competitors brought out very similar ones. Known as 'clones' they are naturally a thorn in the side of the original chip manufacturer.

In a lawsuit the US courts decided that only names, not number combinations such as the logical successor '586' could be trademarked. Any manufacturer could call their processor a 586, and the Intel marketing strategists decided on the name 'Pentium'.

There are other processors in this processor generation. The Pentium II is an extended Pentium processor, which originally comes from Intel and is impressive because of its higher computing power.

MMX is an abbreviation for 'Multimedia Extensions'. It is a special part in the processor which is responsible for the rapid processing of multimedia algorithms.

Perhaps you already own a Pentium MMX. This promises to be of benefit above all to users of games and graphics programs which make special demands on the processor.

The new 'superprocessor' is called 'Pentium Pro' and is currently the most powerful PC processor available.

What to buy: only the best?

A leading processor developer with Intel made the following, apt comparison: 'If the car industry had developed as much as the computer industry, a Rolls Royce would today cost as much as a packet of cigarettes and be the size of a thumbnail.'

This sentence touches on something that makes many users unsure when buying a computer. Naturally the salesperson wants to recommend his (expensive) top model to you, and six months after buying it you find that this top model has now become at best a middle-market model and only costs half what you paid.

For the average user it is certainly not sensible to choose a PC at the top end of the market. In the case of the Pentium Pro the price/performance ratio is anything but favourable, because for the extra price you cannot expect a proportional increase in speed.

At the moment you are probably best to buy a middle-market computer, with a Pentium II processor. To install the latest operating systems like Windows 95 on a 486 computer verges on technical suicide and you'll find yourself in your very own 'wait state' much of the time!

153

Clock rate:
a measurement of speed

So that computing operations can be performed at precisely defined intervals the processor needs a highly accurate time base.

The principle used by the PC corresponds in some ways to the measuring of time with a quartz clock: a crystal passes through a defined number of oscillations in a certain time. A measure of this time base is the clock rate, which is given in 'megahertz' (MHz for short).

The **clock rate** of a PC is given in megahertz (MHz) and is a measurement of the speed of the system.

As a rule of thumb a PC is more powerful the higher the clock rate.

How quickly does an average PC work? While the user of an original PC had to be content with a clock rate of only 8 MHz, the clock crystal of a modern computer manages up to 400 MHz.

You may be able to find out the clock rate of your PC by looking at the case. The clock rate of your computer will be an illuminated segment.

This display is not very reliable because it does not measure the processor's clock ratel. The display is set permanently by the computer manufacturer.

The following exercise shows you how you can find out the actual clock rate of your computer, if you work with Windows NT 4.0.

1 Click the START button, and select PROGRAMS/ADMINISTRATIVE TOOLS (COMMON).

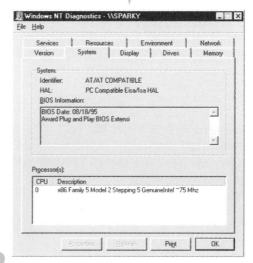

2 Click WINDOWS NT DIAGNOSTICS, followed by the *System* tab.

155

Processor(s):

CPU	Description
0	x86 Family 5 Model 2 Stepping 5 GenuineIntel ~75 Mhz

3 At the bottom of the window that appears you will find an entry 'Processors'. The last sequence of numbers ends with 'MHz' and gives the actual clock rate of your processor.

The bus system as an information superhighway

You may be wondering how the data to be computed gets to the processor and how the result is then outputted to your printer or the monitor.

Clearly the processor has to have a transport system that is comparable with an information superhighway and moves the data between the hard disk, CD-ROM drive, monitor, printer, mouse and any other devices.

WHAT'S THIS?

A computer's data transport system is called a **bus system**.

The way a bus system transports data is technically very complicated. Imagine what is involved in safely transporting data at a clock rate of perhaps 50 or 100 MHz!

The following exercise will, however, give you a feel for the processes in the computer and show you the work of the bus system.

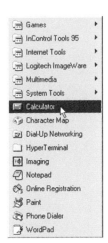

Games ▶
InControl Tools 95 ▶
Internet Tools ▶
Logitech ImageWare ▶
Multimedia ▶
System Tools ▶
Calculator
Character Map
Dial-Up Networking
HyperTerminal
Imaging
Notepad
Online Registration
Paint
Phone Dialer
WordPad

1 Click the START button, and point to PROGRAMS/ACCESSORIES. Click CALCULATOR.

2 The Windows Calculator appears on the desktop. We'll use it to calculate the square root of 1024.

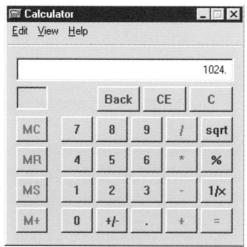

3 Using the keyboard or mouse enter '1024', and press 'sqrt' to calculate the square root.

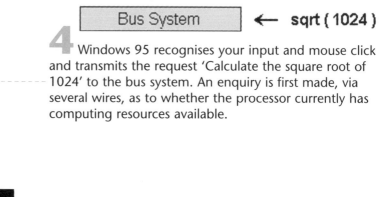

Bus System ← **sqrt (1024)**

4 Windows 95 recognises your input and mouse click and transmits the request 'Calculate the square root of 1024' to the bus system. An enquiry is first made, via several wires, as to whether the processor currently has computing resources available.

Processor ←

Task 1	Task 2	Task 3	Task 4
???	???	???	sqrt (1024)

5 The request now joins a queue of the many other computing tasks the processor has to carry out.

6 The processor works out the result in 32 separate computing steps.

7 The result is now returned to the graphics card via the bus system and shown in the calculator's display. Despite all this, only a fraction of a second elapses between pressing the 'sqrt' button and getting the answer!

There are many different designs of bus systems. Older systems worked with an architecture which was given the name ISA for Industry Standard Architecture as it was an industry-related design.

PCI is the abbreviation for Peripheral Components Interconnect, the current standard bus system.

This bus system is no longer adequate for modern computers as, in addition to a slower data-transfer speed, it has other significant disadvantages. The standard bus architecture used today is called PCI for Peripheral Components Interconnect and was developed by Siemens-Nixdorf.

159

A number of devices connected with the processor are connected to the PCI bus. Besides the printer and mouse, the monitor and expansion modules (which we shall talk about in a later chapter) are also connected indirectly to PCI.

Apart from the high data-transfer rate, PCI has another very attractive feature which makes it stand out. In the past if you wanted to add extras to your PC a technically experienced user or even an expert had to do it for you.

PCI is Plug & Play-compatible, so you can expand your PC's capabilities simply by plugging in a module of this type and then switching it on.

We will show you in detail in a later chapter which extras are useful for your individual requirements.

The motherboard

What is understood in physical terms by a bus system? Several tracks connect the individual components, such as the processor and hard disk, with each other.

The tracks are put side by side on a board. As well as transporting data, the motherboard also performs some other functions, mainly co-ordination ones. So control units and even the processor are placed on the motherboard.

To put as many tracks as possible on a small area – after all computers are getting smaller and smaller – the electrical tracks are laid not only on the surface, but also lower down inside the motherboard.

Because the tracks are as fine as hairs, they can be broken by slightl mechanical strains making the expensive board unusable.

Computer boards are very fragile, so always handle them with the greatest care, and never expose them to mechanical strains!

In earlier chapters we introduced you to some of the most important components that are located on the motherboard.

These include:

- The processor

- The BIOS component

- The clock generator and the internal real-time clock

- Usually, the control unit for the hard disk, floppy disk and CD-ROM drives

- Usually, the various interfaces

- The working memory

- The bus system

161

The world of bits and bytes

In the introductory chapter we explained why a computer works with and calculates in the binary system.

On the next few pages we want to explain in a bit more detail how your computer uses the binary system. This is very important because the whole computer world is based on a numbering system that is alien to most people at first glance.

The bit

The smallest unit of information a computer can process is the 'bit'. A bit can accept the states '0' and '1' and so can be represented, for example, as a magnetic particle on the hard disk or as an electrical 'on/off' switch.

So how many different pieces of information could you represent with these two numbers alone? Only two – zero and one!

It seems at first glance that the binary system is not particularly efficient, as clearly the information content that can be sent with these two states alone is not particularly large.

If, however, only two bits are used much more information can be reproduced. Perhaps you have already assumed correctly that four different states can be expressed, which we have printed below:

1st	bit:	1	1	0	0
2nd	bit:	1	0	1	0

With just one more bit – so a three-bit system – eight pieces of information can be represented:

1st	bit:	1	1	1	1	0	0	0	0
2nd	bit:	0	0	0	0	1	1	1	1
3rd	bit:	1	1	0	0	1	1	0	0
4th	bit:	0	1	0	1	0	1	0	1

If you now assign a letter to each of these four-bit combinations in the columns you can represent 16 states. In other words, the letters A, B, C, and D can be arranged in 16 different ways.

Thus, four-bit system can represent 16 pieces of data, a five-bit system 32. Because we use 26 letters and 10 digits (a total of 36) in normal communication, a six-bit system (= 64 representable characters) should be quite sufficient.

However, the computer uses 8 bits, to reproduce 256 pieces of data.

The byte

A total of 256 different characters can, therefore, be represented in the 8-bit system. This means that a differentiation can be made between uppe- and lower-case letters. In addition sufficient units of information are available for representing country-specific characters (such as accents or umlauts) as well as some punctuation marks and special characters.

A **byte** is another unit in computer technology. It consists of eight bits. The byte is the smallest unit of information for reproducing a number or letter.

The computer combines these 8 bits into another unit, the 'byte'.

The following sequence illustrates how your computer converts a character into a binary sequence and changes it back again before outputting it.

9

1 Using your keyboard type the number 9 which your computer is to add to another number, 2.

**11101010
+
10010011**

2 The computer first converts the number into a binary number and sends it to the bus system which passes on the information.

10010101

3 The processor now adds up both numbers in binary format and returns the result to the bus system in binary form.

11

4 Before it is outputted the calculated binary number is converted into decimal format: 11.

ASCII code

You already know that each binary combination of 0s and 1s is assigned a decimal number. But to which decimal number does the binary number 01001011 belong?

Think what would happen if every manufacturer were to assign these numbers differently: you would type an 'A' on the keyboard, your word processing program could, however, interpret it as 'H', the hard disk save a 'U' and the printer output an 'R'.

Obviously a defined structure is needed which clearly assigns a binary number to a decimal number or another character. One such system is ASCII, by far the most common coding method in the computer industry.

ASCII (pronoucned 'ass-key') is the abbreviation for 'American Standard Code for Information Interchange' and represents a method of coding which assigns a decimal number or character to each binary combination.

ISO and EBCDIC are two other coding methods, but are much less common than ASCII.

Because ASCII code originated in the English-speaking world there were no special characters for other countries (French accented characters and German umlauts, for example) in the early version. The original ASCII code contained 7 bits; the newer version 'Extended ASCII' with 8 bits can reproduce special characters.

165

Quick Progress Check

Main topics: saving and loading

The second progress check deals mainly with disks and how data and files are structured.

➡ Explain the difference between a folder, a file and a drive.

➡ What is understood by the Windows term 'Drag&Drop'?

➡ Give the main advantages of hard disks over floppy disks.

➡ What is a 'head crash', and why is it feared so much?

➡ What is 'formatting', and why do CD-ROMs not have to be formatted?

▱→ What are tape streamers used for? What is their main disadvantage?

_____

▱→ How much quicker is a 100 MHz Pentium than a 50 MHz Pentium?

_____

▱→ Describe the difference between a bit and a byte.

_____

▱→ What does the abbreviation ASCII stand for, and why is this standard very important?

_____

▱→ Name at least five components that are found on the motherboard.

_____

167

What's in this chapter?

First we'll explain which printer fonts are suitable for different purposes and application fields. You will learn the difference between laser, dot-matrix and ink-jet printers, and get to know plotters. We'll also show you parallel and serial printers, and demonstrate how printers send back status signals to the PC. We shall print a document and monitor the printing.

You already know:

Your are going to learn:

169

Computers and paper: inseparably linked?

One main stage in the development of electronic data processing was the efficient management of large amounts of data. No longer did the user have to search for a single piece of paper among bundles or in cupboards full of files, but could request it at the touch of a button on the computer.

Commendable though this stage may be, you will quickly discover from your own experience (or you may have done so long ago) that computers and paper are inseparably linked to each other.

In an earlier chapter, we mentioned the fact that the computer initially caused a real flood of paper. In any event, futurologists are agreed that the 'paperless office' may well remain a vision for ever. According to one insider joke, one page of typed data equals ten or twenty times as much computer-generated paper.

Not all of your business associates have a computer at their disposal, and in any case the different systems are not necessarily compatible with each other, so a large part of correspondence has to be handled with paper.

Apart from communication, printouts are mainly used for archiving databases; these can often be replaced only by means of electronic backup media, because printouts can be read and remain readable irrespective of the hardware used.

The printout instrument used is the printer, whose development has kept up with the PC, like a lot of other equipment. Over the next few pages, we give you first an overview of the development of printer technology. Then we introduce you to some current models of printers, so that you have a good foundation for choosing what to buy.

Printers in the early days

In the early days of computer technology, printers resembled their immediate predecessors, typewriters. But instead of deft fingers being used to enter columns of figures, the computer communicated via a simple interface with the typewriter to put endless amounts of data on paper.

Daisy-wheel printers work like typewriters, but are no longer used nowadays.

These printers were called daisy-wheel printers, because they produced characters with a daisy-shaped type wheel. They are not used nowadays, mainly because they are inflexible, they cannot print out graphics and they are really slow into the bargain.

Their successors used thin metal needles instead of characters. You are probably familiar with this principle from your digital watch, whose individual numbers are displayed with illuminated segments. Similarly, the so-called dot-matrix printers make up individual characters with from 7 to 36 tiny dots.

Dot-matrix printers use metal pins to produce characters in the form of a combination of individual dots.

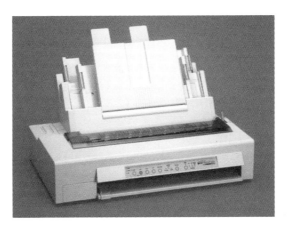

171

The characters which the first dot-matrix printers produced on paper looked rough and disjointed, because the individual dots could be seen with the naked eye. Good quality presentation was therefore out of the question; in this connection, there was much discussion of 'NLQ printers'.

What the customer was promised as 'near letter quality' suitable for commercial purposes and full-bodied, turned out to be of most inferior quality. If anyone were to offer you a second-hand NLQ printer today, you should say no, thanks.

Dot-matrix printers were mainly sought-after because of their ability to print graphics. Because the individual needles could print anywhere on the page, quite complex black-and-white graphics could be produced.

Another disadvantage of the 'needlers' (as they were called in computer slang) was that they are real pains in the neck! The printing noise generated by ten or twenty metal pins is very aggravating, so much so that even soundproofed hoods are commercially available.

However, dot-matrix printers also have their advantages. They are robust, reasonably priced and very fast, and thus offer a cheap alternative for leisure or home use. As they use force to put ink on paper, dot-matrix printers can also produce carbon copies and print on sets of forms (credit transfer forms, tax declarations etc.). So for some business applications, dot-matrix printers are still in use today.

Daisy-wheel and dot-matrix printers are typical impact printers.

Ink-jet printers

The most popular entry-level printer is undoubtedly the ink-jet printer. The underlying technology combines reasonable price with good printing quality.

The print head consists of 24, 48 or more, geometrically arranged jets, through which tiny droplets of ink can be squirted under control. The individual jets are controlled electronically.

WHAT'S THIS?

Ink-jet printers use microscopic drops of ink instead of metal pins. Individual characters are also formed from a combination of individual dots.

Because ink is applied to paper during printing, printouts are liable to smudging. In particular, larger areas of black on paper can cause a wave effect produced by damp ink.

Hewlett Packard, a well-established manufacturer of ink-jet printers uses a special pigment ink. Any printouts produced with this ink give a very uniform effect.

Laser printers

Laser printers, which work rather like photocopiers, are the pinnacle of printing technology. Especially when it comes to printing filigree graphics, laser printers surpass all other printing technologies; they are also suitable for printing correspondence, and produce needle-sharp text documents.

WHAT'S THIS?

Laser printers form characters from colour particles known as toner. They work rather like photocopiers and produce high-quality, high-value printouts.

Laser printers have come down in price to levels that are well within the reach of the home user.

173

The most obvious disadvantage is the high maintenance costs. As well as consumable materials such as the toner and special retaining wires, the exposure drum has to be changed at regular intervals at a cost of up to £100. With good laser printers, the cost of an A4 page can amount to about 6 pence.

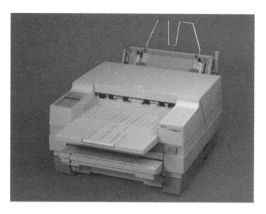

Laser and ink-jet printers are non-impact printers, because they require no mechanical contact with the surface of the paper. This is why no carbon copies or sets of forms can be produced.

Other types of printer

Thermal transfer printers

A few years ago, the thermal transfer print was used exclusively for special applications but, because of certain advantages, it was able to capture a certain segment of the market.

The printhead consists of heatable plates which release a special paint from a coloured ribbon. This paint is absorbed by the paper lying underneath, resulting in a sharp printout. In addition to paper, slides, labels and even textile fibres can be printed.

Thermal transfer printers are mainly suitable for situations where high-quality, high-value prints are required in small quantities. The price of an A4 colour print page can be as much as £1, which is justified, however, by the almost photo-quality realistic colour reproduction.

Plotters

Plotters are not printers in the conventional sense. An electronic adjustment and control unit moves coloured pens horizontally and vertically across a fixed sheet of paper. In addition to the actual movements, there are commands to raise and lower the pens, so that complex graphics can be reproduced.

Plotters are designed for paper sizes ranging from A4 up to A1. At very high prices, they are only suitable for professional use in computer-assisted design.

Serial or parallel?

PC printers are almost exclusively operated from the parallel port. Admittedly they can be operated from a serial port; however, as you will realise from having read the section on 'Interfaces', these operate much more slowly.

Whereas short amounts of text can be produced really quickly on a serial printer, the printing speed slows down when printing any graphics-intensive pages. The parallel port is therefore preferable in every case; the printer manufacturers realise this. Only in exceptional circumstances do they fit their printers with a serial connector.

To be able to exchange data faster between PC and printing system, an expanded parallel-port standard based on the Centronics standard has been developed. This so-called EPP interface facilitates far better data transfer. As long as both computer and printer are fitted with this port, you should be able to make use of the higher data-transfer speed.

EPP is the abbreviation for 'Enhanced Parallel Port', and denotes an expanded parallel port via which the printer can be clearly addressed more rapidly than the conventional parallel port.

175

Status signals

Think back to the chapter 'From human to computer', where we introduced you to the parallel port. There some of the signal contacts passed the printer's status signals.

The printer can obviously send messages back to the PC, telling it that it has run out of paper, for example. The PC informs you of this situation and asks you to insert more paper.

One important status signal which you ought to know about is the 'online signal'. If this signal is active, the printer reports that it is 'ready to print'. Your printer may be fitted with an 'online' button. If you push this while it is operating, the print process will be temporarily interrupted.

Print resolution – a measurement of quality

Remember: All printers form the characters or graphics from individual dots; a dot-matrix printer uses metal pins, the ink-jet printer uses microscopic drops, and the laser printer uses toner particles.

Imagine that you had to make up a particular graphic out of numerous small dots. Naturally, you would intuitively place the dots as close together as possible, so as to obtain a uniform print format. If the dots are placed too far apart on the paper, the individual dots are visible to the naked eye, and the print format creates an uneven and untidy effect.

This is why printer manufacturers aim to place as many dots as possible together on a print surface.

dpi is the abbreviation for 'dots per inch' and is a measurement of the resolution of a printer.

The measurement used for this is called 'dots per inch' ('dpi' for short). This dpi value is a measurement of the resolution and therefore the print quality. It is generally accepted that the more dots the printer can squeeze into one inch, the higher the print quality.

How many dots per inch can be created by modern printers is shown in the following table:

Table of typical printer resolutions

Type of printer	Typical resolution
9-pin dot-matrix printer	150 dpi
24-pin dot-matrix printer	300 dpi
Ink-jet printer	300-700 dpi
Laser printer	300-1,200 dpi
Professional plotters	1,300-4,000 dpi

Colour printers

Although, a few years ago, colour printers were far too expensive for private use, and dot-matrix printers provided print results which at best were barely respectable, since then, colour printers have come down to affordable prices.

Many users content themselves with a black-and-white model when they buy a printer. If you need colour prints, however, colour ink-jet printers are recommended. They work with microscopic ink dots, but can produce millions of colours.

Most colour ink-jet printers have a 'twin-chamber system'. In the first print cartridge – the first chamber – there is black ink, and in the second cartridge there are three chambers filled with blue, red and yellow ink. By carefully mixing these colours, as many as 16.7 million different shades of colour can be produced!

177

The big disadvantage of twin-chamber technology becomes clear when changing the cartridge. Because the three primary colours are stored together in one physical unit, the complete cartridge has to be changed, even if only one primary colour has been used up. This is why many manufacturers now supply four-chamber systems, in which the individual primary colours can be changed separately.

The biggest technical problem in developing colour printer technology was the balance between the screen display and the subsequent printout. In a later chapter, we explain that your screen assembles colours with a completely different system. To convert a certain shade of colour produced by a monitor's colour combination into a colour printer mixture, a complex algorithm is required which is supplied with the printer in the form of a printer driver.

Colour printers based on laser technology provide the best results, but cost at least five times as much as a black and white laser printer, and therefore do not represent a practicable alternative.

Printer languages

The fact that different technologies also involve different standards will come as no surprise to you. You probably already assume that, even within the printer sector, some standards exist which are not compatible with each other.

But after connecting their printer to the parallel port, many users are surprised that, instead of the expected text, only black and white corrupt data are printed out.

All printers at least understand the ASCII character set, which you will remember from the previous chapter. Generic print, another standard that is understood by all printers, is also used in connection with printers.

Remember that, in generic printing, only simple ASCII text can be read. Graphics and special symbols are not transferred properly to paper.

Before you complain to your dealer that your printer is 'defective', you should install the generic printer driver in Windows 95, and then try a simple text document.

The following exercise shows you how to load a generic printer and print a test page in Windows 95. Any other operating system will also offer a generic printer, but its installation may differ in certain cases.

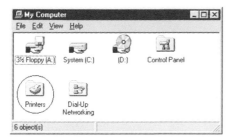

1 Double-click the My Computer icon and find the Printers icon.

2 Double click on the Printers icon. If you have already installed printers in your system, you will find further icons, one for each printer. Select Add Printer by double-clicking on the icon.

179

3 The dialog window Add Printer Wizard will guide you through the installation of the generic printer. Click on Next.

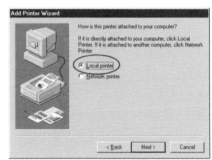

4 In the next window, select the option Local printer.

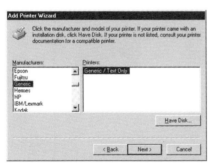

5 In the next window, the type of printer must be selected. In the left pane, choose Generic, and you'll see Generic/Text Only selected automatically in the right pane.

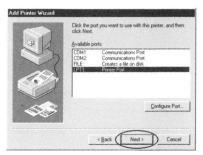

6 Click on Next, select the entry 'LPT1' as the Printer port, and confirm this by clicking the Next button.

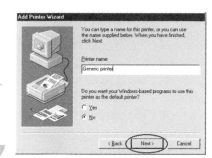

7 Enter 'Generic printer' as the name for the new printer, and confirm by clicking on Next.

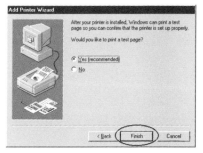

8 Windows 95 finally invites you to print a test page. If your printer is not switched on yet, do so and insert paper. If you now click on Finish, Windows will print out a one-page text document. If the text is legible, you'll know that the printer is correctly connected to your PC.

181

So, where did the afore-mentioned corrupt data come from? To enable a printer to print graphics and other characters not defined in the ASCII code, it must be equipped with a 'higher printer language'.

A printer language or higher printer language enables a printer to print data sent in ASCII code, and thus takes advantage of the printer's capabilities. A printer language is also described as 'emulation' in some cases.

Each printer manufacturer uses their own printer language to 'speak' to their own printer models. A printer driver is then embedded in the operating system. It can be accessed by the application software and the print data can be sent to it.

Fortunately, there are certain 'basic standards' which have been programmed by reputable manufacturers and can be expanded with any special capabilities of a particular printer. This is why you will find several thousand models in the Windows 95 list of printers, even if the underlying drivers differ only in small details.

The following printer language concepts are worldwide in both scope and significance:

The Epson code

The printer manufacturer 'Epson' developed a printer language for dot-matrix printers very early, and called it 'ESCP', meaning 'Epson Standard Code for Printers'. Even today, most dot-matrix printers conform to it, as do some ink-jet and laser printers.

The DeskJet driver

The printer market leader, 'Hewlett Packard' (HP), was one of the pioneers in the manufacture of ink-jet and laser printers, and has accordingly had a lasting influence on these markets.

It was HP who established a general-purpose code for using ink-jet printers. Since then, the example of the 'HP DeskJet' has also been followed by most of the competition.

The LaserJet driver

Like the DeskJet driver, Hewlett Packard has also established a standard for laser printers. Behind the 'HP LaserJet' title lies a universal laser printer language that is understood by many laser printers.

PostScript

The firm 'Adobe' caters for professional users with its printer language 'PostScript', and integrates this language mainly in high-value, high-end printers.

Roughly translated, 'PostScript' means 'after printing'. The principle is far ahead of other techniques, but requires expensive hardware installation. The printer possesses a certain 'innate intelligence' and can independently deal with time-consuming computations which arise prior to printing. As a result, the computer is more quickly available again for other tasks.

Installing a printer driver

To enable your printer to work at its best, a compatible printer driver must be installed. Of course, your printer comes with a set of disks which contain the printer driver.

As an alternative, you can also use the standard printer drivers which are provided by the operating system.

If possible, you should use the set of disks provided by the manufacturer. The drivers they contain are always more up-to-date than the drivers in the operating system and, apart from this, often offer functions which the standard drivers lack.

In principle, the installation of a printer driver is similar to that of the afore-mentioned generic driver, which also takes on a driver function. However, the installation differs in some important respects, so we'll demonstrate the installation of a printer driver for you step by step.

183

If you work with Windows 95, you can still follow the installation, even if you have already installed your printer or if the printer has been pre-configured by the factory. Have the Windows 95 installation CD or the manufacturer's set of disks ready.

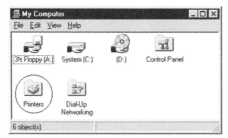

1 Double-click on the My Computer icon, and then select Printers.

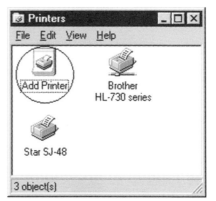

2 Click on Add Printer in order to install a new printer. The already installed generic printer is also displayed in this window.

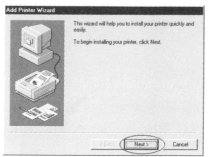

3 Acknowledge the Add Printer
Wizard welcome message
by clicking on Next.

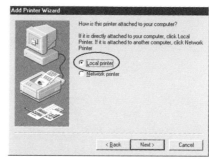

4 Select the option field
Local printer, and go to the
next window by clicking on
Next.

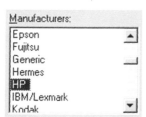

5 If you would like to use the set of
manufacturer's disks, go next to step 7.

If you do not have a set of disks available, select the
(alphabetically sorted) printer manufacturer now,
eg 'Hewlett Packard' ('HP' for short), from the
Manufacturers list on the left..

6 Now select the printer model, eg 'HP DeskJet 310 Printer', from the right-hand side of the window. If your printer is not listed here, you will find further support at the end of this exercise.

Confirm your selection with Next, and go on to step 8.

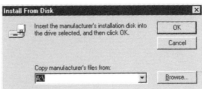

7 Click on 'Have Disk...', and insert the first installation disk from the set of disks. Click on OK. All the drivers stored on the disk are now listed. Click on the driver of your model, and then select Next.

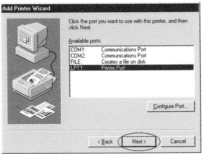

8 Select 'LPT1' as the printer port, and click on Next.

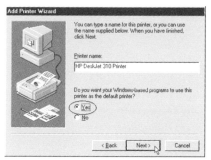

9 In the following field, you can type a name for this printer, or you can use the name supplied. Select 'Yes' so that Windows uses the new printer as the default printer. Confirm the dialog box with Next.

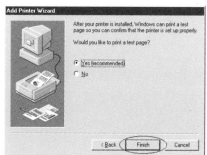

10 Printing out a test page is definitely recommended. So switch your printer on, and insert some paper. Click on Finish. A few seconds later, your printer should start printing a test page.

What do I do without a matching driver?

If you buy a second-hand, older printer, you may have a problem. The disks containing the driver may no longer be available, or the driver may only be suitable for a different operating system.

Moreover, as modern operating systems such as Windows 95 no longer cater for old printers, you cannot fall back on a default printer either.

In such a case, try the following compatible drivers. This way you can at least make use of the most important basic functions of your printer. If you cannot place your printer in one of the categories, try all the printer drivers listed one after the other – you have nothing to lose!

Your printer is a ...	Try the driver for the ...
Dot-matrix printer	Epson FX-80
Ink-jet printer	HP DeskJet
Laser printer	HP LaserJet

Printing documents

Once you have printed out the initial test page as above, the correct installation of your printer is ensured.

You can now carry out an initial test text, format it and then print it out. For this purpose, start any application, open or create a document, and then print it.

If you need a little support, you can turn to the following exercise. First of all, you draft a short text in Windows 95 WordPad, and then print it out.

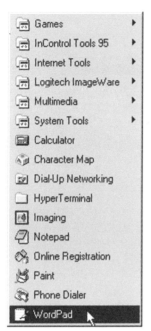

1 Click on the Start button, and select Programs/Accessories/WordPad.

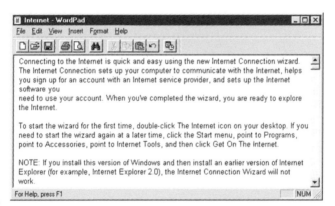

2 Enter several lines of text, which should cover about half a screen. For example, you can copy a few lines from this book.

189

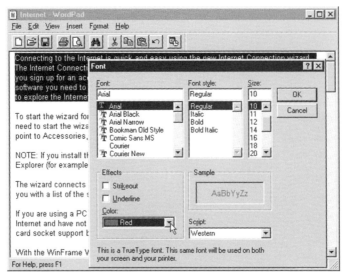

3 If you possess a colour printer, mark any passage of text, and from the Format menu select the command Font. Click with the mouse on Colour, and select the colour Red. The previously marked text is now highlighted in that colour.

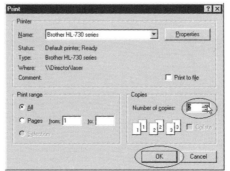

4 From the File menu, select the command Print. Your previously installed default printer can be seen in the Print dialog window. Increase the number of copies to be printed to '2', and click on OK. Printing begins immediately. You should now have two printouts with the same content.

Monitoring printing

All modern operating systems offer you 'batch printing'. You can send several documents from different applications to the printer at the same time and the printer deals with the incoming jobs in a batch.

A printer buffer known as a 'spooler' accepts all printing orders as long as the printer is busy, and passes them on to the printer one after the other.

In batch printing, several application programs can allot printing jobs at the same time. The printing jobs are received by the spooler and relayed to the printer in batches.

You can request the current spooler and printer status at any time. In Windows 95 this is provided by the 'Print Manager', which controls the central coordination of the printer resources in the system.

For example, in 'Windows 95', the following exercise shows you how to examine and manipulate a printing job which has been sent. To follow how this works, your printer must remain switched throughout.

1 Open Windows 95 WordPad by clicking on Start/Programs/Accessories/WordPad.

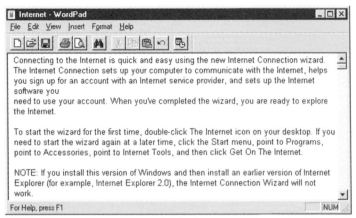

2 Enter about one full screen of text, eg some passages from this book.

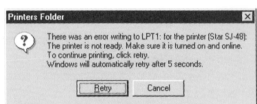

3 Switch your printer off, and from the File menu, select the command Print. Confirm the printing job with a click on OK. Windows 55 now warns you with an error message that there was a problem with sending your document to the printer.

Star SJ-48

4 In My Computer, click on Printers, and then double-click on the icon of your printer.

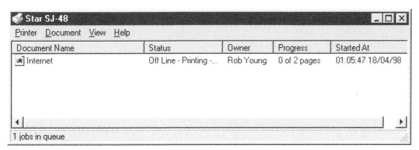

5 The content of the window which opens represents the content of the spooler. Here you find the document which you have just sent to the printer, listed with some extra information.

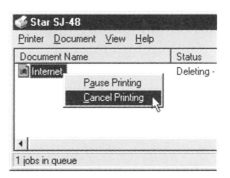

6 Click on the entry for your document. With one click on the Delete button, you can erase the current print job.

193

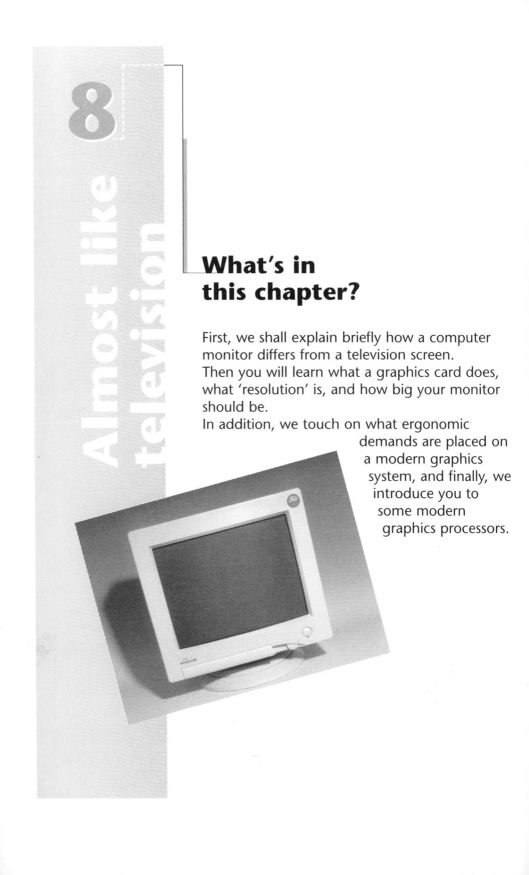

8

Almost like television

What's in
this chapter?

First, we shall explain briefly how a computer
monitor differs from a television screen.
Then you will learn what a graphics card does,
what 'resolution' is, and how big your monitor
should be.
In addition, we touch on what ergonomic
demands are placed on
a modern graphics
system, and finally, we
introduce you to
some modern
graphics processors.

You already know:

Your are going to learn:

195

From the TV to the computer monitor

You have almost certainly worked with it in the previous chapters, and directed your gaze at its illuminated ground glass screen. We are, of course, talking about the monitor, or rather its associated complex graphics system.

The monitor could be regarded as a close relative of the television set, if the areas of application of both devices were not so different. Whereas the television viewer sits further away – about two metres – from the set, the monitor serves as a display unit with which data which have been entered and processed can be checked.

Indeed, every PC could work without a monitor if it were not for you, the user; however, you would be helpless without it, and you could not really interact with the computer. In this sense, monitors are actually superfluous where human intervention is not required. For example, at some sites, network servers are installed without monitors for cost reasons, and a screen is only connected temporarily for maintenance purposes or in the event of a breakdown.

Although the monitor and the television set can only be compared to a limited extent for the reasons stated above, the technical relationship is obvious. In the process of their evolution, computer screens work with technology developed in the video field, but have been enhanced by important innovations.

The graphics card

How does the computer data actually reach your monitor? A 'graphics card' located directly on the motherboard handles the conversion of the image created, and thus acts as the interface between the processor and the screen.

The first so-called graphics cards were – strictly speaking – not 'graphics cards' at all. At best, only text could be produced, and only in one colour. It was only the later generations of graphics cards that were able actually to address individual image points on the screen and so create graphics.

Does this development remind you a little of printers? Here, too, the early typewriters could only produce text, whereas later models such as the dot-matrix printer were also capable of printing graphics.

VGA is the abbreviation for 'Video Graphics Array'. It is the only graphics standard that is currently used.

Modern graphics cards conform to a worldwide standard called 'VGA'. You don't come across this description any more in most specifications or advertisements, because no graphics cards in the PC area conform to any other standards.

Resolution

As with printers, resolution is given in dots with graphics cards and monitors.

Resolution is a measurement of the maximum number of image dots which can be displayed horizontally and vertically.

The more dots that can be displayed, the finer and more faithful to detail the image becomes. However, the resolution of a monitor is not given in 'dpi' as it is with printers, but in horizontal and vertical image points.

A resolution of '800 x 600', for example, means that the screen can display 800 individual image points horizontally and 600 points vertically.

197

Since more image points can be projected onto larger screen surfaces, the resolution of larger monitors is always higher.

You can usually determine how great the resolution of your monitor is from the system software for the operating system. The following exercise shows you how to determine the resolution of your monitor, using 'Windows 95' as an example.

1 Display

Click on the Start button, and select Settings. Select Control Panel, and click on Display.

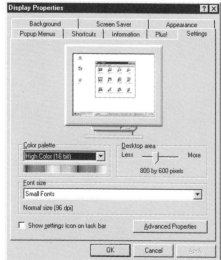

2
A dialog box entitled Display Properties is opened. Click on the Settings tab.

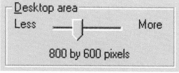

3
In the Desktop area section, the current screen resolution is now displayed for you as the number of 'horizontal by vertical' image points (pixels).

Picture diagonal

The 'picture diagonal' or 'size' of the monitor denotes the measurements of the ground glass screen. This precise definition is therefore particularly important, because the picture diagonal does not necessarily agree with the picture that is actually visible. You are no doubt aware of this effect from the television set; there, too, the actual picture is bordered with black strips of various widths.

Although earlier VGA monitors almost exclusively have picture diagonals of 14 inches (35.5 cm; 1 inch equals 2.54 cm), they have since been superseded by 15-, 17- and 20-inch sets .

In the end, whichever size you decide on largely depends on your personal standards, requirements and budget. However, the spectrum of application software to be used is also important. A 14-inch monitor is definitely not recommended on ergonomic grounds for longer word-processing jobs. For working mainly with graphically-orientated operating systems such as Windows or OS/2, the purchase of a 15- or 17-inch monitor is recommended, so that the graphics, symbols and lettering do not appear too angular and coarse.

Bigger, 20- and 21-inch monitors are sensible only for jobs where great faithfulness to detail is required. In computer-aided design (CAD), for example, it is often important to be able to display a whole A4 page at a time – a difficult undertaking for smaller monitors.

It is generally true that a larger monitor also provides higher resolution, because the dimensions of the tube are greater. The following table summarises the normal resolutions for various picture diagonals.

Table: Recommended resolutions for various monitor sizes

Picture diagonal	Recommended resolutions (pixels)
14 to 15 inches	640 x 480 to 800 x 600
17 to 20 inches	800 x 600 to 1024 x 768
20 and 21 inches	1024 x 768 to 1600 x 1200

199

Picture frequencies: ergonomically important

If you go close to your television set, at a distance of about 30 cm, you will be aware of the picture flickering. The television apparatus renews the visible picture about 30 to 40 times a second; in other words, it has a screen refresh rate of 30 to 40 Hz.

The screen refresh rate (in Hz) indicates how frequently in one second the whole picture is formed.

Imagine that you had to work on a computer with such poor quality for a long time. Headaches would probably be the least health problem you could expect.

Clearly, far stricter ergonomic standards are needed for the quality of a computer screen. This explains the higher price of a monitor and also answers the question frequently asked by newcomers, 'Why can I not use my television set for working on the computer?'

Whereas a TV set works with a screen refresh rate of 30-40 Hz, high-end monitors form the picture at up to 200 Hz, ie about five times as often.

Screen refresh rates of less than 60 Hz are perceived by the human eye as a distinct flickering; working with a 50-Hz system typically causes symptoms of fatigue and eyestrain. These effects only disappear at 70 Hz and upwards, and so, with modern monitors operating at rates of between 80 and 100 Hz, working in front of the screen is in fact ergonomically trouble-free, and thus possible for longer periods.

Table: screen refresh rates and ergonomic working conditions

Screen refresh rate	Working conditions
below 60 Hz	Distinctly discernible flickering
60-70 Hz	Discernible flickering
70-80 Hz	Hardly any discernible flickering
over 80 Hz	Ergonomic area

You can find out the screen refresh rate at which your monitor is working with the system software of most operating systems. The following exercise shows you how to determine and adjust the screen refresh rate of your monitor, using Windows NT as an example.

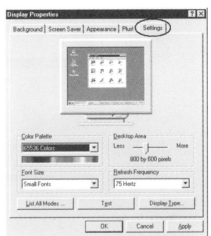

Display

1 Click on the Start button, and select Settings. Select Control Panel, and click on Display.

2 A dialog box entitled Display Properties is opened. Activate the index card Settings.

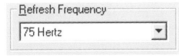

3 In the Refresh Rate section, the current screen refresh rate is now displayed for you in Hertz.

201

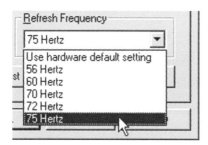

4 Click on the small black triangle on the right, alongside the Hertz number. Further screen refresh rates which your monitor can display are listed here. For ergonomic working you should select 72 or more Hertz.

5 After altering the frequency, click on the Test button. Windows 95 now generates a test picture, which should be clear and perfectly flicker-free.

Driver software

The early VGA standard allowed for a screen refresh rate of only 60 Hz, an area in which ergonomic work was scarcely possible.

So that modern operating systems can exploit the full potential of the graphics card and the monitor, you must install a driver. If you are working with Windows 95, the integrated automatic recognition of a suitable driver has probably already been installed.

You can compare this driver with the already familiar mouse and printer driver. It acts as the interface between the operating system and the hardware, ie the graphics card in this case.

The following exercise shows you how a graphics driver is installed in Windows 95.

Display

1 Click on the Start button, and select Settings. Select Control Panel, and click on Display.

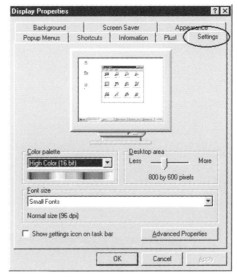

2 A dialog box entitled Display Properties is opened. Click on the Settings tab.

3 Click on the Advanced Display Properties button which is located in the bottom right-hand corner of the window. On the Adapter page, the graphics card and driver being currently used are shown.

4 If you would like to select a different driver, you must know the precise model description of your graphics card. You will find these details in the handbook for the graphics card or for the PC system. Click on the Change... button.

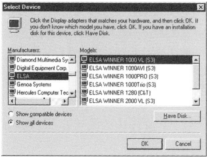

5 From the list of Manufacturers, select the graphics card manufacturer, eg Elsa.

Models:
- ELSA WINNER 1000 VL (S3)
- ELSA WINNER 1000AVI (S3)
- ELSA WINNER 1000PRO (S3)
- ELSA WINNER 1000Trio (S3)
- ELSA WINNER 1280 (C&T)
- ELSA WINNER 2000 VL (S3)

6 In the list of Models, the models of the relevant manufacturer are now listed. Click on the entry for your graphics card, and then select OK.

7 After some files have been copied, you should also ensure that the driver is functioning by clicking on Apply.

Graphics processors

Nowadays, many graphics cards are fitted with their own graphics processor as standard. The steps required for displaying graphics are taken away from the main processor.

Graphics processors are processors specialising in the display of pictorial information which provide their service on efficient graphics cards.

Because the graphics processor is more highly specialised, it can only carry out a few commands specially required for graphics processing, but they are executed somewhat faster than by the main processor.

205

The graphics processor relieves the bus system – as well as the main processor. Whereas the main processor in a system without an intelligent accelerator card has to specify every pixel of a graphic element individually by position and colour, only general terms such as the centre point, radius and colour of a circle to be drawn are needed when working with a graphics processor.

One typical example of a graphics processor is the S3 chip, which is used on many modern graphics cards.

Quick progress check

Main topic: Printers and graphics system

 Via which interface can you connect a printer to a PC? State the advantages and disadvantages.

 What do you call the units of resolution in the printers and graphics area, and what do the abbreviations stand for?

 State the advantages and disadvantages of a dot-matrix printer. Which generic printer must be used if carbon copies are to be created or sets of forms printed?

 What is the 'screen refresh rate', and in what units is it measured? Why must a graphics driver be installed to set ergonomic screen refresh rates above 60 Hz?

What is a graphics processor, and what is its best-known example called? Which two components of the motherboard, in particularly, does using such a processor relieve?

After printing a colour graphic, you establish that the printout is showing colour deviations from the image displayed on the monitor. What is the cause?

Why is the picture quality (and therefore also the price) of a computer monitor much higher than that of a TV set? Which minimum screen refresh rate is recommended for fully ergonomic work?

What is a printer spooler, and why is it used?

What does the abbreviation VGA stand for?

In what sizes are modern VGA monitors available? Why is a 17-inch or larger monitor recommended for working with graphics software?

9

Internet and online

What's in this chapter?

First, we guide you into the 'megamedium' –
the Internet. We show you the difference
between a modem and an ISDN adapter, and
between digital and analogue transmission.
Then we introduce you to the transmission
protocol. We demonstrate how to access the
Internet and discuss the
software needed.

The seventh continent

Very early on, long before the first personal computer was even thought of, some resourceful engineers hit on the idea of joining up several computers into a network.

On 21 November 1969, Professor Leonard Kleinrock was sitting in the information rooms of the University of Los Angeles and typed in the sentence 'Do you see this character?' A few seconds later he received the answer 'Yes' which launched the age of the computer network.

Kleinrock had linked an early IBM computer to a computer 220 kilometres away and transmitted the text via a dedicated line. Nowadays he is regarded as the 'father of the Internet'.

But what is the Internet, that silent time witness that wanders like a ghost through the media? It is often described as the 'seventh continent', as a virtual piece of land. In his novel *New Romances*, the American writer William Gibson talks about a continent whose inhabitants no longer exist physically. He called the continent 'Cyberspace'.

The Internet is a worldwide computer network whose individually connected computers can communicate with each other. It consists of a multitude of cables and a technically defined structure.

It is important to remember that the Internet does not belong to anyone, and is not influenced politically or in any other way. Because the Internet extends worldwide, you can send news and files to any other computer connected to the Internet at negligible cost.

Because other computers prepare data for you, the Internet also acts as the world's biggest information database, whose topicality and speed put every other medium in the shade.

Nowadays, railway timetable information, weather forecasts from the Meteorological Service, online ordering from mail-order firms and customer support can be handled via the 'Internet' medium quicker and more directly than by any other means. Teleshopping and home banking have become as commonplace in the modern household as the coffee machine in the kitchen. You can also obtain the latest software from the Internet which is available as shareware. Communicating with friends and business associates worldwide can take a matter of seconds.

What do you need then, to make your computer suitable for going online?

- A modem or an ISDN card, to process the computer data for the telephone. A modem can be used in any analogue telephone socket. An ISDN card can be used only with a digital ISDN socket.

- Computer software to control the exchange of data between the home computer and the online service; this is supplied with modern operating systems such as Windows 95, Windows NT 4.0 or OS/2.

- A telephone socket for transmitting the data.

The modem: an 'analog bridge'

When data is sent via the telephone network, there is a clash of two different technologies: the digital world of the computer and the, mainly, analog world of the telephone. To bridge these two worlds, a suitable interface, called a modem, is required.

Strictly speaking, a modem is just a converter. The word 'modem' is an abbreviation of the terms 'modulator' and 'demodulator'. It converts the digital signals from the computer into analog (also spelled 'analogue', but more often 'analog' in computer jargon) frequencies (tones) which can be transmitted by the telephone network. Conversely, the demodulator converts these tone sequences into bits which can be recognised by the computer.

The term 'modem' is used when a firm connection to the telephone line exists.

211

By contrast, an acoustic coupler, for example, has no direct link with the telephone network. To be able to work with it, a normal telephone is still needed. The coupler transmits data converted into tones via a loudspeaker into the telephone mouthpiece, and receives the remote station via a microphone or a coil. Thanks to the ever-increasing spread

of mobile phones, with special hardware you can now establish a connection

to online services at any time and almost anywhere.

The choice of a modem should be carefully considered, as it represents the communications interface between you and the online service. A modem that cuts off every second connection because it uses some incompatible firmware will prevent you from making any further calls. An external modem is always preferred to its internal counterpart, because you have the opportunity to monitor your connection by means of the LED indicator lights on the front panel of the modem.

Modems with a data transfer rate of 14,400 bps (bits per second) are the absolute minimum requirement nowadays - and they cost less than £30. If you do not have a modem yet, and you want to decide on which one to buy now, buy a 33,600 bps or 56,000 bps model.

Configuring the modem

Just a few years ago, the user had to configure a modem by typing in cryptic commands taken from the handbook.

Even experienced online experts were almost driven mad by such complex hardware installations. It is no wonder that the user demanded easier alternatives.

As a result, with Windows 95 and Windows NT, the 'plug and play principle' has finally become a reality for modems, too. If you own a fairly up-to-date modem, installation should cause you no problem.

The following exercise shows you how to install a modem with Windows 95. The entire procedure should only take a few minutes.

Modems

1 Select the menu command Start/Settings/Control Panel. Double-click the Modems icon.

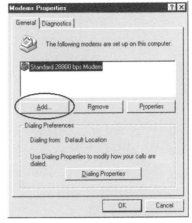

2 In the dialog box Modems Properties, any modems already installed are listed.
Click on Add... in order to install a new modem.

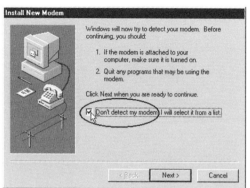

3 The Modem Installation Wizard welcomes you. Switch your modem on, if it is still off. Click on the check box labelled 'Don't detect my modem' and then the Next button.

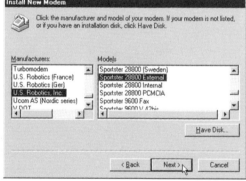

4 Now, you have to select the manufacturer and model. First click on the appropriate entry in the list of Manufacturers. Then select the model in the box on the right. If your modem is not listed, continue with step 5, otherwise go straight to step 6.

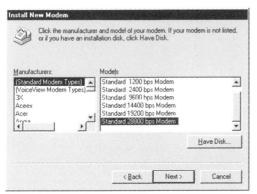

5 As with the general printer driver, several general modem drivers are available to you. If your modem is not listed, select 'Standard Modem Types' as the manufacturer and select an entry with a transmission speed matching yours, eg 'Standard 28800-bps modem' for a 28800-bps model. If you are not sure, select 'Standard 14400-bps modem'.

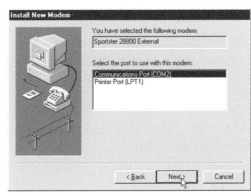

6 Select the port from which your modem is to be operated. This will normally be COM 2.

215

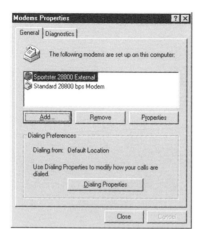

7 After installation, the newly installed modem will be listed in the dialog box Modems Properties.

ISDN: Digital high performance

On an ISDN digital telephone network, the data does not need to be modulated first, but can be digitally transmitted immediately. Instead of a modem, an ISDN card is required for transmission.

In principle, the ISDN card only represents a direct interface between the computer and the telephone network. The ISDN card is addressed like a modem. One prerequisite for such a card, however, is an ISDN socket.

An ISDN adapter replaces the modem in digital data traffic. It acts as the interface between the digital ISDN network and your PC.

The transmission speeds that can be reached here are 64,000 bps; ie more than twice as fast as an average modem. When large amounts of data are being handled, an ISDN connection is more economical than an analogue connection because the running costs of the ISDN connection are also calculated from the same telephone tariff.

Because not all software works directly with ISDN adapters, the ISDN adapter is driven via a 'modem simulator' called cFOS, which causes your system to believe that there is a normal modem present.

WHAT'S THIS?

A cFOS driver simulates a modem to the operating system, so that ISDN adapters can be served as if by normal modems.

The Internet protocol

As we explained to you in the introduction, the Internet is just a collection of various transmission lines. To enable data to be transmitted in this cable system, a defined transmission structure must be present. A so-called transmission protocol forms the basis for a systematic exchange of data. For example, it prepares transmitter and receiver details, as well as checking the integrity of the data being transferred.

Only if all participants work with the same protocol is any orderly data transfer even possible. The protocol used in the Internet is called TCP/IP and is provided by virtually every operating system, including Windows 95, Windows 4.0, OS/2 and any Unix system.

WHAT'S THIS?

TCP/IP is the abbreviation for Transfer Control Protocol/Internet Protocol. It is the transmission protocol of the Internet, and forms the basis of an orderly exchange of data.

The TCP/IP protocol lies, as it were, above the telephone line when you move around in the Internet. You have to install TCP/IP first of all. Windows 95 and Windows NT 4.0 offer special Dial-Up Networking which automatically provides the connection to your service provider and only has to be installed before the first contact.

The following exercise shows you how you install Dial-Up Networking, in order to make contact with your service provider. Installing and configuring the TCP/IP protocol are totally different under various operating systems. You should read the online Help or consult the handbook for the operating system in question.

Until you understand the exercise, keep your service provider's data sheet handy. It was supplied when you registered, and contains the necessary technical details.

Dial-Up
Networking

1 Double-click on My Computer, and select Dial-Up Networking.

2 The connections already installed are now listed. In order to set up a new connection, click on Set up New Connection.

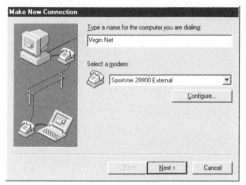

3 In the next window, type an eay-to-remember name for the connection, eg 'Virgin Net', if you are connected to the service provider Virgin Net. In the box marked Select a modem, specify your modem or ISDN card. Confirm your details with Next.

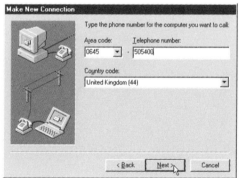

4 Now enter the telephone number with which you can contact your service provider. You will find this on the data sheet issued to you on registering with your service provider.

219

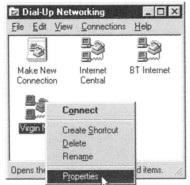

5 When you click on Finish, an icon for the newly made connection is added to the Dial-Up Networking folder. To enter the remaining details, click the icon with the right mouse-button, and select the Properties command from the drop-down menu.

6 Click on the Server Types tab at the top of the window.

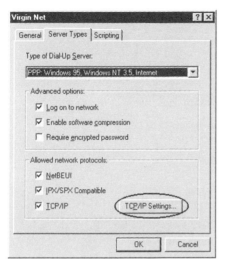

7 The Server types dialog box includes the settings for the TCP/IP protocol. Click on the TCP/IP Settings button.

8 If you have been given an IP address already (see data sheet), this has to be entered in the IP address box. Then click on the options button marked Specify an IP address, and then enter the address in the box provided. Keep the preset IP address allocated by the server handy.

221

Specify name server addresses	
Primary DNS:	255 . 255 . 255 . 0
Secondary DNS:	0 . 0 . 0 . 0
Primary WINS:	0 . 0 . 0 . 0
Secondary WINS:	0 . 0 . 0 . 0

9 If your service provider runs a 'DNS server' or a 'Name server' (see data sheet), some further details are required. Enter the relevant details in the Primary DNS and Secondary DNS boxes. Otherwise, leave that section set to Server-assigned name server addresses. Confirm your details with OK, and close the configuration window.

Your first Internet connection

After you have connected and installed your modem or ISDN adapter, the technical requirements have been met for your first 'surf trip' on the Internet.

You can now set up your first Internet connection via the Dial-Up Networking connection, and thus establish that your settings are correct.

The following exercise shows you how you can set up an Internet connection to your service provider. Whenever you want to go on the Internet, you must follow these steps.

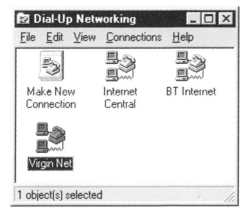

1 Click on the My Computer icon and then double-click Dial-Up Networking. Your connection set up in the previous exercise is now listed here.

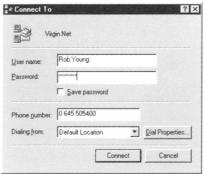

2 Double-click on this icon. A connection window opens, containing the telephone number and some further details. In the User Name box, enter your registered name (see service provider's data sheet). Your password has to be entered in the Password box. In both cases, pay close attention to upper and lower case!
Click on OK to set up your connection.

223

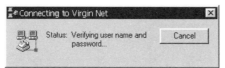

3 A few seconds later, your modem starts dialling. Your computer now reports, User identification is being checked, and Your computer is being registered on the network one after the other. Shortly afterwards, a message briefly appears: Connected at xxx bps, where xxx is the modem speed.

4 To check the connection, you can now double-click on the little modem icon that appears in the bottom right-hand corner of the Windows 95 screen beside the clock.

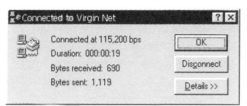

5 The dialog box that appears tell you how long you have been connected to the Internet, and how much data has been sent and received. To hide this dialog again, click the OK button.

6 Click on Disconnect if you would like to break off the connection to your service provider. Windows 95 does not terminate the connection automatically, so you remain connected to your service provider, subject to their charges, until you manually hang up.

Your surfboard on the Internet waves

Just as you need word-processing software to record, edit, save and print text, so the Internet also needs its software.

225

A browser is the underlying software with which information can be obtained from the Internet, and the Internet can be served. It is a 'decoder', so to speak, for the Internet.

The basic Internet software is called a 'browser'. With a browser, you can move around on the Internet, call up information, search through databases, transfer files to your local hard drive and do much more besides.

Whereas there are an immense number of word processors available, in the world of browser software there are really only two popular options: Netscape Communicator 4.0 (previously known as Netscape Navigator) and Microsoft Internet Explorer 4.0.

Whichever software you decide on is up to you. The differences between the two programs for beginners, at any rate, are marginal. They both support a variety of hardware and operating system platforms, including all Windows derivatives, Unix, OS/2 and Apple Macintosh.

Browser software is normally obtainable free of charge. If you work with Windows 95 or Windows NT 4.0, Microsoft's Internet Explorer is already installed on your PC, or is at least located on your installation CD.

Possible reference sources for browsers include:

☞ Computer magazines: Up-to-date browser programs can often be found on CD-ROMs on the covers of specialist periodicals.

☞ Internet service providers: Most of the bigger and super-regional service providers supply a CD-ROM with specialist access software along with the registration documents. There is always at least one browser, if not several, on the CD.

☞ Direct from the Internet: If you have access to the Internet from a different site (through friends, at work, or at university), you can transfer browser software directly.

Look out, there's a data thief about!

Finally, a topic that has received a lot of publicity which should be mentioned here, is Internet security. Data thieves are often talked about; or hackers who cause havoc in the Pentagon; files are allegedly copied from the computer's hard disk, and even bank accounts are reported to have been plundered.

Even though such things are isolated cases, they can cause widespread panic. Many users no longer trust Internet technology. Of course, it is true that the only computers that are wholly safe from intruders are those that are not connected to the Internet. However, it is also true that interference is extremely rare, and sophisticated security mechanisms are increasingly preventing data theft.

If you spend some time on the Internet and take up any online offers with your browser, you should be guided by a certain natural caution.

227

Quick progress check

Main topic: The Internet and going online

⇨ What are the three basic prerequisites to make your computer suitable for going online?

⇨ What is a modem, and which terms go to make up this artificial word? From which PC port is a modem normally driven?

⇨ What is an ISDN adapter, and how does it differ from a modem? Which transmission tasks are optimally carried out with ISDN adapters?

⇨ What is a cFOS driver used for?

⇨ What is an online service? Do you know another expression for this? Name some well-known online service providers.

⇨ What is a transmission protocol required for?

▢➜ **What do the letters TCP/IP stand for, and what lies behind them?**

▢➜ **What is a browser?**

▢➜ **There are two major players in the browser market. Who are they, and in what versions are they available?**

▢➜ **What should be your guiding principle on the Internet, as far as security is concerned?**

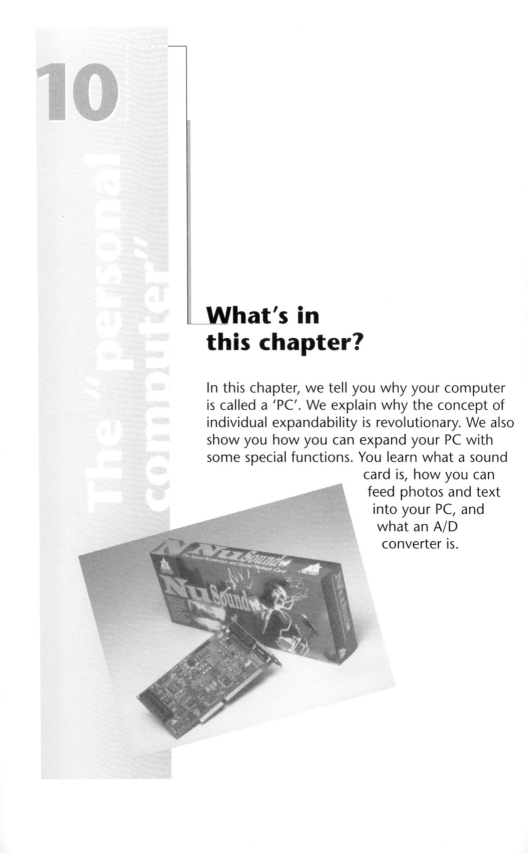

10

The "personal computer"

What's in this chapter?

In this chapter, we tell you why your computer is called a 'PC'. We explain why the concept of individual expandability is revolutionary. We also show you how you can expand your PC with some special functions. You learn what a sound card is, how you can feed photos and text into your PC, and what an A/D converter is.

You already know:

Analog and digital:
two worlds meet   32
Computer language: binary format   38

Your are going to learn:

Your individual PC   232
Interrupt & Co   233
Card drivers   237
Sound cards   239
Optical scanners   240
Network cards   241
A/D conversion cards   242

231

Your individual PC

The experts are agreed: technical superiority alone is not the recipe for success with the personal computer.

The concept of personal expandability was once unique, but it has since been copied by countless computer manufacturers. Every user was meant to be able to assemble his or her computer hardware and software on demand and replace any components that had become too slow with new, higher-performance components.

This ability to adapt to suit the user gave the personal computer – or PC its name.

The first PCs could only display black and white text. Users who required coloured graphics could buy a corresponding attachment. Data carriers that had become too full, such as hard drives, could be replaced with larger mass media.

Nowadays, coloured graphics and large hard drives are standard products. Nevertheless, you can add any further functions which your PC lacks with 'expansion cards'.

With an expansion card (expansion adapter), a PC can be given additional functions with which it is not equipped as standard.

An expansion card consists of an electronic board which is fitted with countless components. Its reverse side fits connectors to the rear wall of the computer cabinet.

The expansion card fits into a socket in the motherboard by means of a multipoint plug, and is thus connected to the bus system.

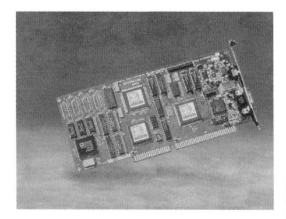

The expansion card is inserted into a slot in the motherboard. It connects the card to the PC's bus system.

With which functions can your PC now be fitted? We introduce you to the most important ones in this chapter. In the following list, you will surely find one or more expansion cards that you might like to install into your PC some time in the future.

Interrupt & Co

Unfortunately, it is not enough merely to insert the expansion card into a slot in the motherboard.

Imagine you are operating three or four expansion cards in your PC. The first one deals with the provision of background music during computer games, the second one connects your PC to a local network, and you are running a weather station as a hobby with the third one.

So that the various expansion cards work together in your PC without any problems, three technical parameters must be allocated to each card. These parameters are independent of the type or function of the card, but only provide PC-internal communication with the card.

I/O port

The card's I/O (input/output) port is comparable with your postal address. An I/O port is allocated to the card, either by small switches on the board before it is installed, or by software after installation.

When the processor now accesses the expansion card, it naturally uses its I/O port. Of course, a card may only be allocated one I/O port, to avoid any confusion.

233

I/O ports are usually recorded hexadecimally, eg '330h' or '220h', where 'h' indicates that this is a hexadecimal number.

Interrupt request

Imagine that you are collecting current weather data with your sample system. The background music card is not being used at this time.

The processor never accesses the installed expansion cards simultaneously, and thus saves computer time. More importantly, it captures data from the cards when these are actually needed. The type of expansion 'asks' the processor, so to speak, if the latter can process the data: it sends an 'interrupt request' (or IRQ) which enables the processor to process the data provided by the expansion card.

Interrupts may be imposed several times only in an emergency; normally only one interrupt per expansion card is required.

Direct memory access

In many cases it is sensible that expansion cards can load data directly into the main memory without the processor's controlling intervention.

Scanners, for example, which feed photographs into the memory, increase their working speed considerably by such means.

The third parameter is therefore 'direct memory access' (DMA for short), which provides the channel via which the data is transferred by the expansion card directly into the memory.

Plug & play

Just a few years ago, and even still today in some cases, the I/O port, the interrupt request and the direct memory access had to be entered manually.

For this purpose, little 'jumper' switches on the card were used to set up different configurations.

This procedure was laborious and assumed a good level of technical knowledge from the user. In the 'plug & play' age, which was brought into being by Microsoft, such configuration work is rarely required.

Plug & play expansion cards configure themselves independently. After installation, they allocate themselves any unused parameters and thus avoid any conflicts with other devices you might have.

The following exercise shows you how to read out the parameters already reserved for the interrupt request, the I/O port and the direct memory access under Windows 95.

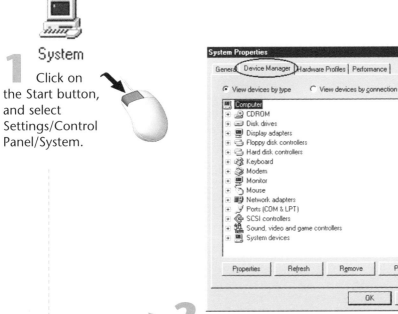

System

1 Click on the Start button, and select Settings/Control Panel/System.

2 The System Properties dialog box is opened. Select the Device Manager tab in which the installed expansion cards, sorted by category, are listed.

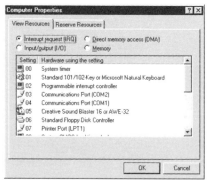

3 Double-click on the top entry, 'Computer'. A dialog box opens, showing you the current interrupt settings. The 'Setting' column contains the IRQ value, and the 'Hardware using the Setting' column shows you the corresponding expansion card.

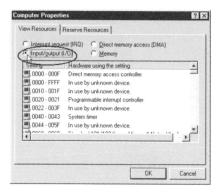

4 Click on the Input/output (I/O) option box. This window contains the I/O port currently reserved by your PC system.

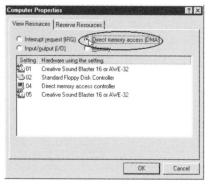

5 Click on the DMA option box. The channels reserved for Direct memory access are listed one after the other.

Card drivers

Just like the mouse, printer and graphics card, every expansion card needs a special card driver. This driver communicates with the card; therefore it has to know the values for the IRQ, DMA and I/O port.

Plug & play systems recognise many drivers for more recent expansion cards, and connect them immediately after they have been installed and the PC has been switched on for the first time.

And right after the hardware recognition, which was explained earlier, Windows 95 installs a suitable driver.

An expansion card does not work without a suitable driver, even if the correct values for DMA, IRQ and I/O port have been installed correctly.

The following exercise shows you how to find out the hardware settings and drivers used by a particular device in Windows 95.

1 System

Click on the Start button, and select Settings/Control Panel/System.

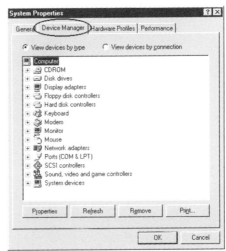

2 The System Properties dialog box is opened. Select the Device Manager tab in which the installed expansion cards, sorted by category, are listed.

237

```
□ ⅏ Sound, video and game controllers
       ⅏ Creative Advanced Wave Effects Synthesis for AWE 32
       ⅏ Creative Sound Blaster 16 or AWE-32
       ⅏ MPU-401 Compatible
```

3 Now select the category under which
you'd expect to find the desired expansion
card listed. For example, if you would like to
check your sound card, double-click on
'Audio, video and game controllers'.

Creative Advanced Wave Effects Synthesis for AWE 32

4 All devices in this category are now
listed. Double-click on the
desired expansion card, eg the
sound card.

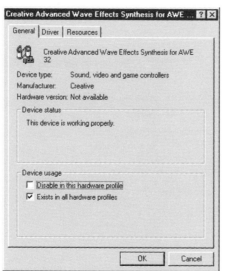

5 The General tab contains some general
details about the card, eg the information
'This device is working properly'. Here you will
also find a detailed fault list if the expansion
card does not work.

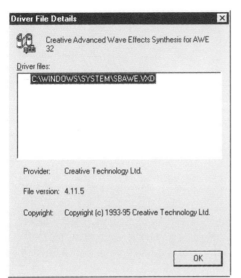

6 Select the Driver Tab and click the button labelled Driver File Details. The installed driver is now listed, and the entry 'File version' gives you the version number of the driver.

Sound cards

Gone are the days when a PC drew attention to itself by means of an internal loudspeaker, especially when being switched on, and perhaps when a fault occurred.

The trend towards multimedia applications and operating systems demands one thing more than anything else, apart from sufficient processor performance: sound. This word denotes any sound humanly perceived in the form of music, tones or noise.

Of course, the loudspeaker which is still included in every PC does not provide any sound of the quality desired by the user. As an expansion adapter, a 'sound card' expands your PC with the relevant potential, and is often the first expansion card that many users buy.

239

Every computer game is supported by a dozen different sound cards at the same time; this is an indication of the apparently diverse equipment used to generate sounds and music. The sound quality of newer games is excellent. Realistic effects provided as background music of CD quality and with Dolby

Surround Sound no longer places any great demands on the equipment. The interactive cinema atmosphere is now within everybody's reach.

However, there are vast differences in the capabilities of the various sound adapters fitted, in the technical potential, and in price, of course. Whereas a simple and inexpensive sound card is perfectly adequate for PC games, you obviously have to dig deeper into your pocket for multimedia applications or for semi-professional sound editing.

Optical scanners

A 'scanner' is used for feeding in graphic images. A sensitive and precise optic – similar to a photocopier – scans an image, eg from a book or a periodical, and sends the pictorial information obtained to the PC.

By using the appropriate software, the scanned image can be stored on a hard disk and printed. Powerful graphics applications such as Corel Draw or Micrografx Designer make image enhancement simple. Effects such as distortions and mirror images are possible, as is enlarging or minimising the picture or masking any unwanted parts of it.

A second major use for a scanner is computer-controlled character recognition.

Complete pages of text, such as a book or a newspaper, can be scanned in, just like a picture. Special programs can recognise the characters and convert them into a text document which you can then edit with a word processor such as WordPad.

An image whose text is to be recognised must be clean and clearly legible, so that any spots do not cause recognition errors. One other prerequisite is that the letters and numbers must be typed; the recognition of handwriting is not yet possible within the bounds of PC technology.

Network cards

If you use your PC in your office, you may want to hook it up to an existing local network. A 'network card' will connect your PC to the network.

There will then be an outlet from your PC to which the network cable can be connected, so that the link is established with the network.

Even with plug & play systems, the installation and connection of the network card may need to be carried out by network specialists, because your PC has to be configured correctly to adapt to the peculiarities of the network.

A/D conversion cards

Finally we would like to introduce you to a card that will satisfy practically all your desires in its range of functions. In science and technology, 'analog-to-digital converter expansion cards' are used very frequently.

You are already familiar with the basic technology from the earlier section of this book in which we explained the difference between analog (or analogue) and digital signals to you. Analog signals – noises – are converted into digital information which can be stored as bits. A/D converters are used in other areas, too, usually unbeknown to the user. A modem is another example of a device with which analog signals have to be converted into digital ones.

The range of applications for A/D converter cards is extraordinarily wide. Some frequently used fields of application are as follows:

 Measuring voltage and current. An A/D converter can be used to determine voltage and current.

☞ Determining chemical conductivity using A/D converters. Chemical conductivity can provide information on levels of industrial waste pollution, for example.

☞ Measuring speed. In automotive engineering, stroboscopic flashing lights are used to determine engine speed.

☞ Specifying weather data. Analog signals involved in determining wind speed, level of precipitation and temperature are converted into digital information for use in weather analysis.

What's in this chapter?

We conclude our journey together through the PC world with a chapter on software. We explain the various kinds of software and the differences between individual programs. You learn why software is sometimes provided free, or can be very expensive. We show you some important standard applications, eg programs to record texts or to create graphics.

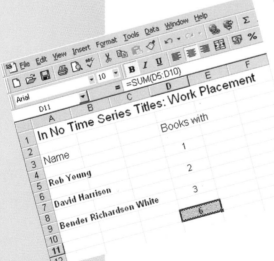

You already know:

Your are going to learn:

Nothing happens without software!

The most powerful and modern PC can scarcely be of use unless it is equipped with the relevant software.

You have already got to know some software while studying the last few chapters: Windows 95, WordPad, Word for Windows and Explorer.

Application software is taken to mean any software that supports you in your work. In this chapter, we would like to introduce you to the most important software types and give you an overview of current programs.

Standard software

'Standard software' means any programs that you can obtain from a computer dealer or shop. It is comparatively expensive, but is not adapted to your individual needs.

Standard software is used for the basic functions that are required by most users. It includes word processors as well as graphics programs, spreadsheets and database programs.

Horizontal software

Standard software which is subject-specific, and is thus limited in its field of application, is called 'horizontal software'. Typical examples of this type are bookkeeping and accounting software.

Vertical software

Software that offers comprehensive functions for one subject, is usually written by smaller specialist firms. 'Vertical software' is always very expensive, but can be adapted to individual requirements on request.

Typical PC users who install vertical software are doctors, lawyers and insurance brokers.

Individual software

If you are not lucky enough to find the right software for a specific task among the types outlined above, you can have the software written for you by a programmer.

This individual software is exactly tailored to your requirements, and can be modified at any time on demand. Of course, individual software is very expensive; for some programs, you might pay tens of thousands of pounds.

Software packages

Complete software packages include several individual applications which complement each other in their functions. The best-known example of this is probably Microsoft Office, which includes word-processing software, a database program, a spreadsheet and presentation software. IBM also produce a similar package of applications called Lotus SmartSuite.

The data exchange between the individual modules is often standardised, so that addresses from a database, for example, can also be retrieved into the word processor very easily.

If you add up all the individual prices of the components included, there is a considerable cost saving. Office packages often form the basis for useful daily tasks, because word processing, database access and spreadsheets are required by most PC users.

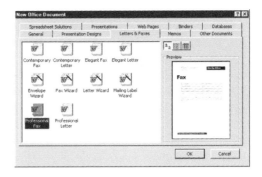

Light versions

Light versions are software products whose range of functions has been reduced. If you work only infrequently with spreadsheets and only need basic functions to calculate a table, you can ask for a light version. Light software is much cheaper, and if you want to buy the normal version (the 'full product') later on, you only have to pay the price difference.

Bundled software

If you buy hardware or a new computer system, you will often find bundled software among the packaging. These programs are provided by the hardware manufacturer in addition to the component or PC system. For this purpose, the manufacturer has agreed a special contract with the software manufacturer.

Shareware, public domain and freeware

Another kind of software includes shareware, freeware and public domain products.

In many cases, this software is completely free of charge. You obtain such programs, for example, via the Internet, from friends, in the supermarket or from various CD-ROMs. Freeware and public domain products are free and you can use them without restriction.

Shareware is often reduced in its range of functions, or can only run for a limited period (normally 30 days). If you like the program, you can register it with the author by paying for it and receive an unrestricted copy. If you don't like it, of course, you just stop using it and don't pay a penny.

Word processors

The most frequently encountered software on any computer is probably the word processor. You can use it to type text, edit it later and format, save and print it.

Modern word-processing software offers some very efficient functions. Complete books (this one, for example) can be produced with it. Page numbering is also possible, as are headers and footnotes, the compilation of circular letters, indexes and contents lists, automatic checks on spelling and even grammar.

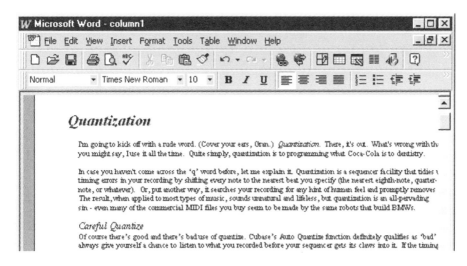

A word processor which covers the basic functions is bundled with most operating systems, including Windows and OS/2. Advanced functions, however, cannot be expected of them.

Major word processors are Microsoft Word, Lotus WordPro and Corel WordPerfect.

249

Spreadsheets

With spreadsheets, the screen is divided into columns and rows. You can enter numbers in the cells formed, and connect the cells with each other by means of calculations.

In this way, you can compile invoices, estimate financial plans with debit–credit analyses, calculate interest and display the results as charts and graphs rather than plain figures.

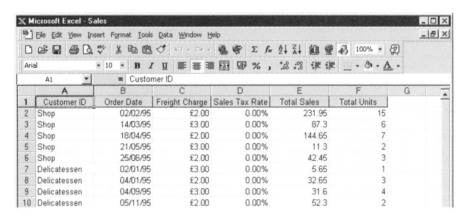

	A	B	C	D	E	F	G
1	Customer ID	Order Date	Freight Charge	Sales Tax Rate	Total Sales	Total Units	
2	Shop	02/02/95	£2.00	0.00%	231.95	15	
3	Shop	14/03/95	£3.00	0.00%	87.3	6	
4	Shop	18/04/95	£2.00	0.00%	144.65	7	
5	Shop	21/05/95	£3.00	0.00%	11.3	2	
6	Shop	25/06/95	£2.00	0.00%	42.45	3	
7	Delicatessen	02/01/95	£3.00	0.00%	5.65	1	
8	Delicatessen	04/01/95	£2.00	0.00%	32.65	3	
9	Delicatessen	04/09/95	£3.00	0.00%	31.6	4	
10	Delicatessen	05/11/95	£2.00	0.00%	52.3	2	

Major spreadsheets are Excel by Microsoft, 1-2-3 by Lotus, and Quattro Pro by Corel.

Database software

Databases handle addresses, appointments, delivery deadlines and itemised data, as well as stamp collections or other private details. With powerful search engines, you can search the database or have sorted lists compiled in accordance with search criteria.

In a so-called 'mask', you can define a formula into which later data can be entered. In the individual fields of the mask, calculations can also be carried out. If, for example, a minimum order total or a minimum stock figure is not reached, the database can report this on demand.

Graphics programs

With graphics software, you can draw colour graphics and combine them with other elements such as text. Virtual drawing instruments such as a paint brush, eraser and pencil, an air brush spray gun and filling functions are available.

Many graphics programs include a 'clip art library' containing many ready-made pictures and graphics. In this way, you can easily design invitations or letterheads.

With graphics software, photos that you have fed into your PC with a scanner can also be edited. You can adjust the contrast and the brightness, remove parts of the picture or add new graphic detail to them.

Popular graphics programs are Corel Draw, Adobe PhotoShop and JASC's Paint Shop Pro.

Quick progress check

Main topic: Software

 1. Name at least two programs that are bundled with Windows 95 which we have introduced you to in earlier chapters.

2. Why is 'standard software' very expensive?

3. What is meant by 'bundling software'?

4. What is 'individual software' and what are its characteristic features?

5. What is the difference between freeware and shareware? And what is 'registration'?

6. What are 'light' versions, and what is meant by a 'full product'?

7. Name two popular word processors.

8. Name three major areas of application for which database software is suitable.

9. You would like to present your quarterly sales statistics in graphic form to the board of directors. What kind of software would be suitable for this?

10. What is an 'office' package? Name two major products.

Useful information

Solutions to 'quick progress checks'

Progress check on 'input devices and interfaces'

1. The standard is called MF-II.

2. A code page contains country-specific information. It is loaded when the operating system is started up, and remains in the background while it is working. With its help, PCs can be used in various countries without having to restructure the hardware.

3. a) and b) activate various functions in conjunction with other keys; c) cancels the current operation; d) switches over to 'insert' mode; e) moves the cursor to the beginning of the line; f) moves the cursor to the end of the line; g) prints the current screen; h) are assigned various user-defined functions.

4. In a mouse, the movement of a ball is converted into a movement of the screen pointer. With a joystick, a control column activates contacts, which is converted into up/down and left/right movements.

5. A mouse driver converts the electrical signals generated by the mouse into information to be interpreted by the operating system.

6. To the first serial port, COM 1.

7. Two serial ports (COM 1 and COM 2), one parallel port (LPT 1) and the game port (GAM).

8. With serial communication, only one bit of information is transferred at a time, whereas parallel ports transfer eight bits at the same time. Parallel ports are therefore much faster.

9. It operates the joystick.

Progress check on 'saving and loading'

1. A file contains information. Files can be kept together in a folder which is stored in a data carrier.

2. By using drag & drop, objects can be quickly moved from one position to another.

3. Hard disks are faster, and can hold larger amounts of data.

4. In a head crash, the read/write head touches the surfaces of the data carrier. All data stored on the hard disk are thus destroyed.

5. In formatting, a structure is imposed on the data carrier. With CD-ROMs this is not necessary, because optical media are involved.

6. Tape streamers are used for backing up large quantities of data. Magnetic tapes must be rewound if various data are to be accessed.

7. Double the clock frequency also means double the working speed within a processor class.

8. A byte contains eight bits.

9. American Standard Code for Information Interchange. Using this code, data can be exchanged between incompatible devices.

10. Clock, processor, memory, bus system, real-time clock.

Progress check on 'Printers and graphics system'

1. Printers can be connected to the serial or the parallel port. Parallel communication is much faster, but shorter distances between PC and printer can be bridged.

2. 'dpi' (standing for 'dots per inch') for printers, and 'dots per row by dots per column' (in pixels) for graphics.

3. Dot-matrix printers are robust, reasonably priced and can print sets of carbon copies. However, they are noisy and the print is of poor quality. If carbon copies are to be produced, dot-matrix printers must be used.

4. The screen refresh rate indicates how frequently the screen is newly formed in one second. The unit is Hz (Hertz). Because rates of no more than 60 Hz are allowed for in the VGA standard, a graphics driver is required for ergonomic screen refresh rates.

5. A graphics processor can carry out graphics operations independently. The best-known example is called S3. A graphics processor relieves the main processor and the bus system.

6. Printer and monitor work using different colour-mixing processes. This leads to slightly deviating results.

7. Users sit nearer to the monitor and also work in front of the PC for longer than they watch television. A screen refresh rate of 60 Hz is ergonomically required.

8. A printer spooler accepts data allocated for printing by the application software, and passes it to the printer in turn.

9. Video Graphics Array.

10. Typical sizes are 14, 15, 17 and 20 inches. Because the resolution and thus the faithfulness to detail increases with larger screen diagonals, sizes of 17 inches or higher should be used for graphics applications.

Progress check on 'The Internet and going online'

1. A telephone line, a modem or ISDN adapter and communications software are required.

2. A modem transmits digital information via analog lines. 'Modem' is made up from a combination of 'modulator' and 'demodulator'. A modem is always operated from a serial port.

3. An ISDN adapter is the interface between the PC and the digital ISDN network. They can transmit at rates of 64,000 bps.

4. A cFOS driver simulates a modem when an ISDN adapter is used.

5. An 'online service' (or 'service provider') provides you with access to the Internet. Examples are CompuServe, AOL, MSN and Virgin Net.

6. The transmission protocol controls the data transfer.

7. Transfer Protocol/Internet Protocol. They indicate the Internet transmission protocol.

8. A browser is the basic software of the Internet.

9. Microsoft Internet Explorer and Netscape Communicator, both in version 4.0.

10. Adopt a degree of caution, and refrain from any behaviour which you would refrain from in any other circumstances.

Progress check on 'Software'

1. WordPad and Explorer.

2. It can be sold in large quantities, so that the unit price drops.

3. 'Bundling software' is enclosed with hardware products or PC systems.

4. This software is written individually to meet your requirements. It can also be modified later to suit any possibly changed circumstances. As a result, it can be very expensive.

5. Freeware is completely free whereas, with shareware, a fee (the registration fee) is charged when the trial period expires.

6. Light versions are versions which have been reduced in their range of functions. The full product includes all functions on offer and is obtainable as an upgrade.

7. Microsoft Word, Lotus WordPro, Corel WordPerfect.

8. Recording addresses, stockholdings and numbers of items.

9. Spreadsheets provide the desired function.

10. An 'office package' comprises several individual applications which are frequently used in daily office work. Examples are products by Microsoft ('Office') and Lotus ('SmartSuite').

File extensions

In chapter 3, we introduced you to file extensions and their purpose. At that point, we listed some typical and frequently used extensions.

On the following pages, you will find a comprehensive table of the most significant file extensions.

Ending	Abbreviation for	Program	Meaning
$$$	Temporary file	Various programs	Temporarily stored auxiliary file
1ST	First	Various word processors	First information. Read first!
ARC	Archive Compression	ARC (Archiving program by System Enhancement Association)	Compressed data archive
ARJ	Archive R. Jung	ARJ (Archiving program-shareware by Robert Jung)	Compressed data archive
AVI	Audio-video interleave	Video for Windows (Windows expansion by Microsoft)	Audio/video document
BAK	Backup file	Various programs	Backup copy of a file
BAS	Basic file	eg Quick Basic by Microsoft (including MS-DOS)	Contains the source text of a basic program
BAT	Batch file	MS-DOS	Batch file contains DOS commands

Ending	Abbreviation for	Program	Meaning
BMP	Bit map	eg Microsoft Paint (included in Windows)	Non-compressed bit map graphics
CDR	Corel Draw	Corel Draw (vector-orientated drawing program)	Vector graphics
CFG	Configuration	Various programs	Program configuration
DAT	Data	Various programs	Data file
DBF	dBase File	dBase database	Data file
DLL	Dynamic Link Library	Windows or OS/2	Object library
DOC	Document	Word processors, eg Microsoft Word and WordPad	Text document
DRV	Driver	Various operating systems	Device driver
EPS	Encapsulated PostScript	Various vector-orientated programs	Graphics file
EXE	Executable	Various operating systems	Executable program
FAQ	Frequently Asked Questions	Various text viewers	Text file with 'frequently asked questions' (and answers)
FAX	Fax	Various fax programs	Fax document sent or received
FOX	FoxPro	FoxPro database by Microsoft	Data file

261

Ending	Abbreviation for	Program	Meaning
GIF	Graphics Interchange Format	Various graphics programs	Compressed graphics file
HLP	Help	Microsoft Windows and applications	Help document for the online help
HTML	HyperText Mark-up Language	Any WWW/ Internet browser	Hypertext document
ICO	Icon	Microsoft Windows	Little graphic symbol
IDX	Index	Various databases	Index file
INI	Initialisation file	Various programs, including Microsoft Windows	Initialisation configuration
JPG	Joint Photographic Group	Various graphics programs	Compressed graphics file
LOG	Logfile	Various programs	Protocol file
MID	MIDI	Various music programs	MIDI music file
MOD	Module	Various music programs	Sound module
MOV	QuickTime movies	Various video playback programs	Video file
MPG	Moving Pictures Group	Various decoder programs	Compressed video file
PAS	Pascal	Programming languages Turbo Pascal or Delphi	Source code
PCD	Photo CD image	Kodak photo CD viewer	Graphics file

Ending	Abbreviation for	Program	Meaning
PCX	Pixel file image	Various graphics programs	Graphics file
RTF	Rich Text Format	Various word processors	Formatted text document
SCR	Screen saver	Microsoft Windows	Screen saver
SIK	Backup copy	Various programs	Backup copy of a file
SWP	Swap file	Microsoft Windows	Swap file for Windows
TMP	Temporary file	Various programs	Temporarily stored auxiliary file
TXT	Text	Various word processors	Text document without formatting
XLS	Excel spreadsheet	Microsoft Excel	Table

Disk formats

The following table shows you the disk formats used today:

Format	Capacity	Disk type		Density
5¼- inch	180 Kb	Single-sided,	single-density	48 TPI
5¼- inch	160 Kb	Double-sided,	double-density	48 TPI
5¼- inch	1.2 Mb	Double-sided,	high-density	96 TPI
3½- inch	720 Kb	Double-sided,	double-density	135 TPI
3½- inch	1.44 Mb	Double-sided,	high-density	135 TPI
3½- inch	2.88 Mb	Double-sided,	high-density	96 TPI

263

Processors

The following table lists the original Intel processors:

Designation	Bit width	Maximum clock frequency
8088	8-bit	9.54 MHz
8086	16-bit	10 MHz
80186	8-bit	8 MHz
286	16-bit	25 MHz
386 SX	32-bit	40 MHz
386 DX	32-bit	40 MHz
486 SX	32-bit	66 MHz
486 DX	32-bit	50 MHz
486 DX2	32-bit	80 MHz
486 DX4	32-bit	120 MHz
Pentium	64-bit	233 MHz
Pentium II	64-bit	400 MHz
Pentium Pro	64-bit	200 MHz

How long should cables be?

In chapter 2, in the section about parallel and serial ports, we showed you that, to transport data free from interference, cables must only be of a certain length. Some further maximum lengths of frequently used cables are given in the following table:

Purpose of use	Maximum length
SCART	Maximum approximately 3m
RS 232	Up to about 100m Highly immune to interference (but then no more maximum transmission rates) Specification, however: maximum 15m
Parallel cable	Maximum approximately 5m (and up to 20m for some devices)
Monitor	Maximum approximately 3m (very susceptible to interference)
Telephone	Up to 500m for extensions

Popular operating systems

In chapter 1, you were introduced to some operating systems. The following table provides information about the most frequently installed operating systems in 1996:

Designation	Manufacturer	Installed versions
Windows 95	Microsoft	45,727,000
Windows 3.1x	Microsoft	20,902,000
Mac OS	Apple Macintosh	5,395,000
Windows NT Workstation	Microsoft	3,448,000
MS-DOS	Microsoft	2,041,000
OS/2	IBM	1,899,000
NetWare	Novell	606,000
Windows NT Server	Microsoft	550,000
Unix	Various	373,000
Others	Various	166,000

265

1st-level cache

The first-level cache is the integrated cache memory which is found in some 486 and in all Pentium chips. It accelerates the work of the processor with an 8 Kb, 16 Kb or 32 Kb section.

2nd-level cache

The second-level cache is fitted to the motherboard. It is used as the actual cache memory between the normal main memory and the processor. Its size varies from 64 Kb up to 1 Mb.

A

Accelerator card

A PC plug-in card which, being equipped with its own integrated processor, is optimised for carrying out some functions particularly quickly. Graphics accelerator cards which are specially fitted for operating under Windows are often used. As a result, the processor is relieved, and the image compilation is accelerated.

Advanced Power Management

APM is a power-saving function implemented in the BIOS which takes over the management of the hardware (hard disks and monitor). Hardware which supports this standard can usually be switched to different power-saving modes (eg standby or complete shutdown).

Aliasing

If images are processed at too slow a scan rate (resolution) during digitalisation, this can cause aliasing (image imperfection) as a result of edge formation.

Analog

Unlike digital data processing, not only are the conditions zero and one possible here, but a whole series of interim stages. As a rule, analog (or analogue) signals are not as exact as digital ones, but can accommodate more information. Telephone conversations (apart from ISDN usage) are transmitted as analogue signals. Computers work internally with digital data.

ANSI

Abbreviation for American National Standards Institute. The ANSI code specifies a series of screen display control commands, and is especially important in data transmission with a terminal program.

Anti-aliasing

This technique reduces the alienation of images caused by **aliasing** by smoothing out any sharp edges.

API

Abbreviation for Application Programming Interface. The API is a standard interface via which the programmer can make direct use of the functions of the operating system (eg Windows).

267

ASCII

Abbreviation for American Standard Code for Information Interchange, a character code on a 7-bit basis. The ASCII code is used by virtually every PC. The expanded, 8-bit code is frequently used nowadays. As a result, besides the standard characters, special characters and country-specific characters have also been added. Altogether 256 characters can now be used (as opposed to 127 with the 7-bit code).

ASPI

Abbreviation for Advanced **SCSI** Programming Interface. The expanded driver interface is for use by the SCSI controller.

Asynchronous

With asynchronous data transmission, the transmitter and receiver alternate with the transmission. After receiving the data, the receiver confirms correct receipt, while the transmitter waits for this signal before sending the next data (cf **synchronous**).

ATAPI standard

Abbreviation for Advanced Technology Attachment Packet Interface. The ATAPI specifies a standard in accordance with which devices other than hard disks, eg CD-ROM drives and tape streamer drives, can be operated.

AT Bus

Abbreviation for Advanced Technology Bus. Another expression for the IDE bus system.

Autopark function

Modern hard disks automatically 'park' their writing and reading heads at the edge of the disk when the computer is switched off, so that no traces of data can be damaged in the event of a dreaded head crash. Older hard disks had to be manually moved into this parking position.

AV-optimised

Abbreviation for Audio-Video optimised hard disks. When playing back audio or video sequences on the computer, this sometimes resulted in intermittent operation with conventional hard disks. AV-optimised hard disks are equipped to provide continuous data flow without any interruptions.

B

Bad clusters

Physically faulty sectors on a hard disk are identified in a list as bad clusters, so that these parts can no longer be used by the operating system.

Bandwidth

The frequency width of a data transmission path (normally the telephone line). A high bandwidth enables several signals to be transmitted simultaneously. At roughly 600 Mbits/sec, fibre-optic cables are currently the most efficient transmission paths.

Bank

A bank is a series of memory components which is addressed via a data line. To expand the memory, any individual bank has to be completely used up first. Earlier, memory banks with no more than 4 Mb were commonplace; nowadays steps of 8 Mb or 16 Mb are required.

Bank switching

For this simple form of memory administration, the memory is divided into memory banks which are administered separately.

Basic Input/Output System (BIOS)

The BIOS makes a computer's basic input and output functions available. It is ready immediately after the PC is switched on, and manages the collaboration with the resident operating system. The CMOS-RAM is evaluated for initialisation.

Baud rate

The baud rate specifies the physical transmission speed, which should not be confused with the data transfer rate. A modem with a speed of 28,800 **bps** works only at 2,400 to 3,400 bauds. In practice, not much higher values than this can be reached on an analogue telephone line.

Beep code

Because errors can sometimes occur (eg motherboard errors), even in a self-test, which make any screen display impossible, the result of the test is given by the PC's internal loudspeaker. The type of error can be identified according to the length and number of the individual beeps.

Benchmark

A procedure which gives a comparable standard for assessing the performance of a computer system in a run-time test. The most important features here are: running time, memory capacity reserved and hard disk performance.

Beta version

The various development stages of any software are often designated with Greek letters. A beta version is the first really operational version after the alpha version. It is still liable to errors and is presented to a restricted panel of testers for assessment in normal operation.

Binary

The name of a two-value counting system in which the only conditions possible are zero and one. Computers use this system for internal processing (cf **digital**).

BIOS

Abbreviation for Basic Input/Output System.

Bit

A bit contains digital information, and can have the condition 'on' or 'off', corresponding to one or zero (cf **byte**).

BNC jack

A plug screw connector for a twin-core cable. It is used for network connections, for example, or for connecting an RGB monitor.

Board

A synthetic plate to which the electronic components are soldered. By means of a chemical etching procedure, the board holds electricity-conducting circuits to which the individual components are connected. The biggest board in the computer is the motherboard, but all plug-in cards also consist of boards.

Boot sector

The boot sector of a data carrier (hard disk or floppy disk) contains the physical details of the memory medium, as well as details of the programs to be started up first.

Bootstrapping

The name given to the procedure which the computer carries out when it is switched on, prior to loading the actual operating system.

bps

Abbreviation for bits per second. The number of bits transmitted per second measures the performance of a data transmission system.

Buffer

Memory that is used for short-term interim storage of data. Such data can be managed according to different models (eg LIFO, FIFO).

271

Bug

As the first computers still worked with relay switches, it could happen that a small insect (bug) would block such a switch. A tedious search was then made for the source of the fault. Today, programming errors are named after these tiny creatures.

Burn-in

A durability test for a computer is called a burn-in test. As the probability of error increases with the increased warming-up of a component, certain thermal errors do not show up until after running for 24 or 48 hours.

Bus

The various components of a computer system are connected to a bus. Data and control signals are exchanged via this bus, which consists of several parallel leads.

Bus mouse

The exotic bus mouse is driven by a special expansion card instead of the normal serial port. It has the advantage that no COM port is occupied, but it requires an expensive plug-in card (not to be confused with the PS/2 mouse).

Bus system

A bus system is a system of parallel leads. It is used for transmitting data between the individual system components, particularly the plug-in cards.

Byte

A byte consists of two half-bytes each containing four bits. With 8 bits, 28 different bit patterns, ie 256 characters, can be displayed.

C

Cache

A component used for the interim storage of data. Frequently used data that would otherwise have to be newly read every time by a slower medium (eg by the hard disk) is stored here temporarily. In this way, it can be fetched from the RAM memory with significantly reduced access times. In addition, larger areas can be read at the same time. This is quicker than reading the data one piece at a time because the reading head, for example, has to be continually repositioned. In that case it is also important that the correct strategies are used to read the data that is required next. Besides the hard disk cache, there is also a processor cache. This uses faster memory components in order to store the contents of the slower RAM memory there temporarily. (See also **Hit**).

Caddy

Caddies are protective plastic cases for CD-ROMs. They protect the sensitive discs from scratches and dust. The CDs are inserted with their caddy into special CD drives. As a result, there is no need to remove the CD from, or replace it in, its case.

Calibration

Fluctuations in temperature can result in minimal changes in the size of the highly sensitive magnetic disks on a hard disk. This could result in data tracks not being read properly, because their position had changed. For this reason, modern hard disks have a re-calibration function. The read/write head moves to a fixed position, and then determines its position relative to the disk surface by reading the data. After a procedure lasting about 0.5-2 seconds, the work can be resumed.

273

CAPI

Abbreviation for Common API. The CAPI is a software interface required for internal ISDN cards. The communications software used falls back on the CAPI functions of the driver to use the ISDN plug-in card. There is a difference between the older version 1.1 CAPI, which is suitable for the national ISDN, and the newer version 2.0 CAPI, which supports the newer Euro ISDN.

CD-A

Abbreviation for Compact Disc – Audio. CD-A is the name used for 'normal', conventional, audio music CDs.

CD-I

Abbreviation for Compact Disc – Interactive. The CD-I standard has been developed jointly by Philips and Sony specially for interactive video applications in CD-ROM format.

CD-R

The CD-Recordable involves a write-once CD-ROM (WORM).

CD-ROM

Abbreviation for Compact Disc Read-Only Memory. The familiar CDs from the music field, but used for data storage, are described as CD-ROMs. Unlike the music CD, it also holds further information for fault diagnosis, as well as data. A CD-ROM has a total capacity of 682 Mb.

CD-ROM-XA

This standard is an expansion of the normal CD-ROM for combining diverse data (audio, video and computer data) on one disc.

Centronics interface

The printer interface (principally the parallel port nowadays) has been virtually standardised by the firm Centronics. The present-day printer interface, however, allows for a significantly higher data transfer rate.

CE standard

Since the beginning of 1996, all electronic devices or components have had to comply with the rules of Conformité Européenne in accordance with the legislation of the European Union.

Cluster

A cluster is defined by the MS-DOS operating system as the smallest indivisible unit for storing data on a hard disk. Depending on the size of the hard disk, eight or more sectors form a cluster. In floppy disk drives, the number of clusters and physical data tracks is the same, as their number here is still very small (2,880 on a 1.44 Mb floppy disk).

CMOS-RAM

Abbreviation for Complementary Metal Oxide Semiconductor. CMOS specifies a technique for manufacturing integrated circuits. The basic information about the hardware configuration is stored in the PC's CMOS-RAM. The data stored in the CMOS is assessed and processed by the BIOS.

Convergence

In a monitor, convergence denotes the correct relationship of the three primary colours red, green and blue. If this relationship is not correct, white lines or edges may be produced, for example; the picture then becomes blurred.

CPU

Abbreviation for Central Processing Unit. The CPU specifies the processor, the core of any PC (eg 486 or Pentium).

Crosslinked files

When files are managed with an **FAT**, system crashes can often result in some parts of files being incorrectly linked. However, this can often simply involve previously deleted data, and usually the files can be fully restored by using a special program (eg ScanDisk).

275

Cylinder

Hard disks consist of several magnetically coated disks arranged one above the other. Each individual disk is divided into tracks that run in circles round the central axis, and are divided again into sectors. The tracks of the disks arranged one above the other are combined in cylinders.

D

D/A converter

Abbreviation for Digital-to-Analog Converter. This component converts digital information into an analogue signal (the opposite of the analogue-to-digital converter). In the CD player, for example, the digital PC information is converted into analogue acoustic signals.

DAC

Abbreviation for Digital-to-Analogue Converter. Graphics cards, for example, have a DAC for converting digital display information into analogue monitor signals.

DAT

Abbreviation for Digital Audio Tape. A tape system that has recently made a big entrance into the computer world as a backup medium. One major advantage over other tape standards (eg QIC) is the very reasonably priced tapes, as they are manufactured in considerably greater numbers.

Daylight-saving time

Most newer BIOS versions offer a choice of this option. It ensures that the change-over from winter to summer time is made automatically. Windows will display a message telling you that your system time has been changed to take account of the switch between British Summer Time and GMT.

DCI

Specially to accelerate video applications and games running under Windows 3.1x, Intel and Microsoft have developed the standard Digital Control Interface (cf DirectDraw).

DDC

Abbreviation for Display Data Channel. Information is exchanged between the monitor and the graphics card via this standardised channel. This exchange is significant for energy-saving measures, for example, as well as for supporting the plug & play function.

Degaussing

Monitors in the higher-price and -quality bracket often have a degaussing button. With this button, the picture tube can be demagnetised. In rare cases, excess magnetisation can lead to slight colour shifts.

Dhrystone

This special benchmark test particularly tests the performance of the processor. It also tests how often the CPU can carry out certain minor programs (Dhrystones) within one second.

DIL

DIP components are also often described as Dual In-line (DIL) Chips.

Digital

The opposite of analogue.

DIP

Abbreviation for Dual In-line Package. A DIP housing is a certain kind of chip design in which two rows of pins are located at the longer outer sides. In contrast, an SIP (Single In-line Package) has only one row of pins.

277

DIP switch

With the DIP switch, some very small switches are enclosed in a plastic housing. Normally several switches are found together in one housing. They are used for adjusting certain options, eg for printers or on motherboards, and can usually be moved with a pointed object.

DIN

Abbreviation for German Institute for Standardisation (based in Berlin). In the areas of communications and data processing, the DIN has its own committees who establish standards in accordance with an established procedure. The Institute's terms of reference range from the standardisation of interfaces and the determination of specialist terms to collaboration with other standardisation institutes (eg CCITT).

DirectDraw

Principally to accelerate games and graphics applications under Windows 95, Microsoft developed the DirectDraw standard. To be able to use it, the relevant drivers for the graphics card must be installed.

DLL

Abbreviation for Dynamic Link Library (cf **Library**).

DMA

Abbreviation for Direct Memory Access. With DMA procedures, the data streams between the peripheral devices and the working store are initiated by the processor, but then subsequently handled by the DMA controller. The DMA is thus used not only to relieve the processor, but also to provide significantly faster data transfer. Control is exercised by up to eight DMA channels, so that each channel is dedicated to one (DMA-equipped) peripheral device.

Dongle

A dongle is a copy-prevention plug-in device. It is connected to a computer port (usually the parallel port) so that it can be read by the computer. A dongle normally contains a particular individual code. This code is requested by the relevant program.

If there is no dongle available, the program will not start. As each program version sold is supplied complete with such a dongle, this would indicate a pirate copy. For reasons of cost, using a dongle is only economically viable with expensive professional applications.

Double-speed drive

A CD-ROM drive with 'double' speed works at a data transfer rate of about 300 Kb/sec. (cf **QuadSpeed**).

DOS

Abbreviation for Disk Operating System. DOS denotes the operating system which is suitable for interacting between the individual components and gaining access to the memory medium. In everyday speech, however, the MS-DOS operating system is referred to as DOS.

dpi

Abbreviation for dots per inch. It represents a unit of measure for resolution. A normal ink-jet or laser printer, for example, prints with a resolution of 300 dpi.

DPMI

Abbreviation for DOS Protected Mode Interface. This software interface standardised by Microsoft provides programs with additional memory of up to 4 Gb by switching the processor into protected mode.

279

DPMS monitor

Abbreviation for Display Power Management Signalling. For this energy-saving function, the correspondingly equipped graphics card can lower the power consumption of a DPMS monitor at various stages.

DRAM

Dynamic RAM: **RAM** memory components, whose information has to be renewed at regular intervals (at a 'refresh rate') (cf **SRAM**). The DRAM components in the PC normally have to be refreshed at 15-microsecond intervals.

Driver

Drivers are programs which run in the background and take over the control of certain hardware components (eg the graphics card).

DSP

Abbreviation for Digital Signal Processor. Used on video or sound cards, it relieves the computer's CPU of the calculation-intensive digitalisation tasks.

Dual-port

Dual-port memory components have two separate input and output buses. They can therefore be written and read at the same time. This technique is mainly used in memories for high-value graphics cards (cf **VRAM, WRAM**).

Duplex

Duplex drive represents a data transfer procedure. Information can be both sent and received on only one data channel (also called full duplex). There is also half-duplex operation.

DVD

Abbreviation for Digital Video Disc. A further development of the CD-ROM, specially for video applications. It can apparently hold up to 17 Gb of data in MPEG-2 format on one CD.

E

ECC

Abbreviation for Error Correction Code. ECC RAMs not only recognise bit errors, but can usually also correct them independently. However, because of their high costs, they are only used in extremely security-critical areas.

EDC

Abbreviation for Error Detecting and Correcting (synonymous with ECC).

EEPROM

EEPROM is the latest further development of **EPROM**, a permanent read-only memory whose data can be erased. In this case, however, the information is not erased by UV light, but electronically. So this does not have to be done with a special device, but can be executed within the computer. Such ROM components are also described as flash memory, and are used, for example, as flash BIOS in the PC. The BIOS version here is accommodated within an EEPROM, and can be easily updated whenever there are version changes.

E-IDE

The Enhanced IDE interface is an expansion of the normal **IDE** standard. Unlike the capacity of the IDE system, which is limited to 504 Mb, the bounds of the enhanced standard have been expanded to 7.8 Mb. In addition, as many as four hard disks (rather than two, as hitherto) can be driven by one controller. The E-IDE standard is fully compatible with IDE devices.

E-ISA

Abbreviation for Extended ISA, a further development of the **ISA bus** standard from a 16-bit to a 32-bit system. It was mainly used with the 386 processor, but was soon superseded by the **PCI** system. The E-ISA was fully upwards-compatible, but could still use the old ISA expansion cards. However, because of this necessary compatibility, some compromises had to be accepted during development.

EMM

Abbreviation for Expanded Memory Manager. This program, which is part of MS-DOS, manages the expanded working memory in accordance with the EMS specifications on 386 computers and upwards.

In addition, it enables the upper memory areas to be used, especially for device drivers and memory-resident programs.

EPP

Abbreviation for Enhanced Parallel Port. This is an expansion of the normal parallel port. It enables data transfer up to twenty times faster. One great advantage of the EPP technique is that it is fully upwards-compatible, and can also be used with the old printer. Such fast ports are offered almost exclusively nowadays.

EPROM

Abbreviation for Erasable Programmable Read-Only Memory. This is a PROM, a programmable read-only memory which is also fully erasable. The erasing is usually done with UV light which shines through a window built into the chip.

External cache

This externally stored cache memory is usually referred to as the second-level cache, located on the motherboard.

F

Fast ATA

Besides the **E-IDE** bus, the firm Seagate has further developed the ATA standard into Fast ATA. Fast ATA does not require any additional hardware, but can reach data transfer rates of up to 13 Mb/sec in **VLB** or **PCI** systems. This standard is fully compatible with the **IDE** bus.

Fast ATA 2

This system, which is once again fully upwards-compatible, is a further development of the Fast ATA standard, and can increase the data transfer rate to as much as 16 Mb/sec.

Fast page mode

In fast page mode – a further development of the paging technique for memory management – it was possible to increase the speed even further. If there is a change to another page and therefore a change to a new line, this change-over is accelerated by special coding. This technique, also known as FPM for short, is used as the main memory in normal **DRAMs** nowadays.

FAT

Abbreviation for File Allocation Table. The MS-DOS operating system (and its further developments right up to Windows) typically manages files on floppy disks and hard disks with the FAT. The file allocation table is a kind of index of contents. For each cluster on the data carrier, it contains a precise record of its content. In addition, the individual clusters are linked to each other by this list. If a file extends over several clusters, for example, the FAT will refer to the next cluster each time. Of course, when storing a file, the file system tries to reserve clusters that are adjacent to each other. However, if this is impossible because of a lack of space, a file can end up being scattered all over the disk. This is known as fragmentation. One big disadvantage of the system is that, in the worst case, any damage to the FAT can result in the total loss of the data. This is why DOS basically always makes a second copy of the FAT.

FCC

Abbreviation for Federal Communications Commission. This American authority tests electronic devices for the interference they emit. For computers and their peripherals, the limitations for class B digital devices apply, in accordance with part 15 of the FCC guidelines. Accordingly, the device must not cause any harmful interference, and must cope with any interference affecting the device.

Feature connector

The feature connector is an optional connector found on most higher-quality graphics cards. It is designed for further graphics-processing add-on cards which have to work with the graphics card directly. This mainly involves video-processing cards. Unfortunately, such interfaces are not always completely matching, so that only certain cards will fit together.

FIFO memory

Abbreviation for First In/First Out memory. With this memory, the data first stored is also the first to be read (straight-through memory). In this way, managed memory can be used as temporary storage for printer output, for example (cf **UART**, **LIFO**).

File sharing

Access to a file by several programs at the same time. This function is only required in multitasking operating systems or on a network. Care must be taken here to provide sufficient protection to separate the files, so as to avoid the loss of any data. For this purpose, MS-DOS offers the command SHARE.

Firmware

Most of the more complex peripheral devices require controlling software built into the ROM (from the motherboard to the printer). This software, contained in the ROM and stored by the device manufacturer, is also called firmware.

Fixed-frequency monitor

A monitor which, unlike the multi-frequency monitor, can only be operated at a single fixed frequency and screen resolution.

Flag

A marker, a changeable variable that can be used to indicate particular states. A flag can be set, erased or read and thus also highlight certain states.

Flash BIOS

A device that uses an **EEPROM**, or **Flash PROM**, to store the **BIOS**.

Flash PROM

Another name for **EEPROM**.

Floptical

Abbreviation for Floppy optical, a flexible optical storage unit. Comparable with a floppy disk, the data here is also stored magnetically. Apart from that, however, the read/write head is kept exactly on track with a laser beam. As a result, a significantly higher number of tracks is possible. A floptical disc the size of a conventional 3½ inch floppy disk can hold up to 20.8 Mb.

FM

Abbreviation for Frequency Modulation, a procedure for artificially creating almost real sounds.

FPU

Abbreviation for Floating Point Unit. FPU is the name of the mathematical co-processor, which considerably speeds up operations with floating decimal points. In modern processors (486 DX and upwards), a unit for faster execution of such operations is invariably built-in already.

285

Fragmentation

Fragmentation is a typical problem of the **FAT** filing system. In the worst case, individual parts of a file are located in individual clusters scattered all over the hard disk. Reading such data takes considerably longer than if the files were all located on the same track, one after the other. This disjointed storage can be corrected with the relevant tools (which are included with Windows). Defragmentation should be carried out at regular intervals.

Frame

Term often used in the computer field to denote a partial area in a larger amount of data. In addition, a 'frame' can be a single image in a video sequence.

G

Games card

The games card or games port is a plug-in card specially designed for computer games, and contains a joystick connector. Nowadays, an individual card is no longer required for this connector, as it is built-in as standard, for example into a sound card.

GDI

Abbreviation for Graphics Device Interface. The GDI is a Windows-supported printer interface. Only the printing technology is built into the printer itself. The internal processor and memory required to prepare the data are missing. These functions must therefore be taken over by Windows. The advantage is that GDI printers are much smaller and cheaper to build. The big disadvantage is that the devices only work under Windows, and so occupy both computer time and PC memory during printing.

GLSI

Abbreviation for Giant Large-Scale Integration. GLSI denotes the degree of integration of a chip. At this level, more than 1,000 million transistor functions can be accommodated in one chip.

GND

Abbreviation for Ground. This is the American expression for the electrical earthing of a cable.

Green function

Another name for the environment-friendly energy-saving mode APM.

GUI

Abbreviation for Graphical User Interface. Unlike systems offering a command control via text input, a GUI provides significantly easier access to functions. The most important functions can usually be intuitively reached with a mouse. Examples of GUIs are Windows or OS/2.

H

Half duplex

Half-duplex operation represents a data transfer procedure. Here, information can only be sent or received simultaneously on one data channel. In contrast to this is **duplex** operation.

Hayes standard

The company Hayes have made the control of modems with AT commands into a quasi-standard, as a result of their widespread use and high quality. Even today, all currently used modems are Hayes-compatible.

287

Head crash

The head of a hard disk normally moves over the magnetic disk without touching it. In the event of any disturbance, caused for example by a jolt, the head will briefly touch the magnetic track and thus destroy most of the data. A head crash, however, can also be caused by a single speck of dust, as the gap between the disk and the head is very small.

Hertz

Frequency (oscillations per second) is specified in 'Hertz', a unit of measure. It is named after the German physicist, Rudolf Hertz. The clock speed of the processor, for example, is given in Megahertz (MHz).

Hexadecimal

This counting system, based on 16, is used for the simpler illustration of binary numbers. Thus, an eight-digit dual number can be expressed with a two-digit hexadecimal number. In the computer area, such a number is often used to specify a memory address.

HFS

Abbreviation for Hierarchical File System. In contrast to the **FAT** file management system, Apple Macintosh computers, for example, work with the HFS procedure.

Hidden files

Most operating systems make it possible for any files to be made 'invisible' to the user. Hidden files still exist, and can still be called up, but can no longer be seen in Windows Explorer and its equivalents. This option offers a small degree of security against inquisitive associates, but can be very easily bypassed or reversed.

High Colour

In contrast to **True Colour** display, only one 15- to 16-bit depth of colour is used here. The palette of colours thus contains 32,768 or 65,536 colours. This depth is adequate for an almost true-to-life display with a correspondingly higher processing speed.

High-resolution

A screen resolution containing more than 800 x 600 pixels is described as high-resolution (hi-res).

High Sierra standard

The first definition of a CD-ROM standard was called High Sierra standard. The ISO 9660 was based on this.

Hit

If the data in the cache memory match the data which have just been requested by the processor, and can therefore be loaded directly from the cache memory, this is called a hit.

Host adapter

The SCSI controller is also called the host adapter.

HPFS

Abbreviation for High-Performance File System. The HPFS is the procedure with which the OS/2 operating system manages its files.

In contrast to the standard management with an **FAT**, it makes storage possible without any extensive **fragmentation**. In addition, it allows file names which are longer than the standard eight characters.

HPGL

Abbreviation for Hewlett Packard Graphic Language. The HPGL is a graphics and printer language developed by the firm Hewlett Packard. Its work is vector-orientated, and has now developed into a standard, eg for laser printers.

I

IC

Abbreviation for Integrated Circuit. An IC is a silicon chip on which a complete circuit has been mounted in a complicated procedure (eg memory components or processors).

Ice cap

Trade name for one of the first processor coolers. The original ice cap consists of a Peltier cooling element with a fan mounted on top. Simple imitations often dispense with the electrically driven cooling element. Cooling is normally advised for all processors with a clock frequency of more than 33 MHz.

iComp

Abbreviation for Intel Compare. Processor comparison test introduced by Intel and used mainly in its own advertising. It was meant to create a particular overview of the growing range of products for Intel processors. In the absence of any comparative details of processors made by other manufacturers, no true comparison is possible.

IDE

Abbreviation for Integrated Drive Electronic. The IDE standard, also known as the AT bus, identifies a hard disk standard. In contrast to other procedures, the controlling electronics is located on the hard disk.

Hard disks with IDE electronics are connected to a simple IDE controller which is often already integrated into the motherboard nowadays.

Indeo

Abbreviation for Intel Video, a standard introduced by the firm Intel to compress digital audio and video information (similar to **MPEG-2**).

Interface

An interface is a hardware or software component used for the exchange of information between different components (cf **API**). In order to be able to connect a printer to a PC, for example, the data from the computer have to be sent in standardised form. This can only be done with a suitable interface.

Interlace

The interlace or field procedure option is the now out-of-date possibility of being able to display higher image resolutions on low-performance hardware (graphics card, monitor). The monitor beam is controlled in such a way that it alternates between displaying only the odd- or the even-numbered lines at any one time in a single sweep. However, as a result, the beholder is given the clear impression of a flickering picture. Present-day systems enable sufficiently high screen refresh rates to be achieved in non-interlaced modes also.

Interrupt

By using the special interrupt lines of the bus system, the processor's work can be interrupted to enable it to see to other tasks for a short time. Software and hardware interrupts are differentiated according to the source of the interruption. For example, moving the mouse triggers an interrupt, as the movements have to be displayed on the screen immediately without having to wait for the end of a process.

I/O card

Abbreviation for Input/Output Card, a plug-in card responsible for various data input and output functions.

IOS

Abbreviation for Input/Output System. The IOS is the part of an operating system which is responsible for the input and output functions. In MS-DOS, this is mainly handled by the IO.SYS components.

IRQ

Abbreviation for Interrupt Request. This signal to interrupt is triggered by peripheral hardware. Altogether, a PC bus has a limited number of eleven IRQ lines.

ISA bus

Abbreviation for Industry Standard Architecture bus. The ISA bus is a standardised PC bus which was originally developed by the firm IBM in 1987. This 16-bit bus system has gained acceptance as a standard for PC-compatible devices and, thanks to its easy expandability by means of plug-in cards, has made a major contribution to the great success of the PC. Both ISA and its successor **E-ISA** have been superseded by the 32-bit PCI.

ISDN

Abbreviation for Integrated Services Digital Network. The ISDN integrates the digital transfer of data and speech. A simple ISDN connection already contains two channels, and thus enables data to be transferred at 64 bps. It is connected to the PC with a simple and very reasonably priced ISDN plug-in card.

ISO

Abbreviation for International Organisation for Standardisation. It covers the standards institutes of about ninety countries nowadays (cf DIN).

ISO 9660

An international standard that regulates file records on CD-ROMs. In particular, it deals with the location of data, directories and their number, and file names.

J

JAZ drive

A further development of the **ZIP drive**. It is a kind of alternative disk drive. The individual storage media offer a capacity of 512 Mb or even 1,070 Mb. Its speed has also been increased by comparison with the ZIP drive.

JPEG

Abbreviation for Joint Photographic Expert Group. The JPEG standard is a compression procedure for digital images. The procedure achieves very high compression rates while it abstracts similar shades of a colour. The loss of quality involved is relatively small. For professional applications, however, this procedure is unsuitable, as it is not capable of producing the original state from the compressed file. Here, too, no true compression procedure is involved, but rather a reduction procedure.

Jumper

Jumpers are little plug-in, dipole bridges with plastic sheathing. On hard disks or older graphics cards, for example, they are used for activating or deactivating certain functions, or for installing interrupts.

K

Key lock

By using a key-operated switch on the PC cabinet, the keyboard can often be electrically separated from the computer, thus preventing unauthorised access.

Kilobyte

One kilobyte (1Kb) corresponds to 1,024 bytes.

293

L

Landmark

The landmark test is a well-known benchmark test which determines the performance of a PC, particularly its **CPU**.

Landscape

A printout format in which the page is printed crosswise, across its longer side.

Library

A file in which closed program functions are kept for use by the various programs. In this way, standard routines do not have to be newly developed every time. In Windows, such libraries are called DLLs.

LIFO memory

Abbreviation for Last In/First Out memory. The last information stored is the first to be read again (batch memory). (cf **FIFO memory**).

LPT

Abbreviation for Line Printer. The LPT port denotes the output interface designated by the operating system for the printer (as a rule, the parallel port).

M

Main board

Another name for the **motherboard**.

Mapping

The allocation of logic sectors to the physical sectors of a memory medium is described as mapping. Mapping is principally necessary for reasons of compatibility. A hard disk, for example, can thus simulate a different sector division from the actual physical one.

MCI

Abbreviation for Media Control Interface. The MCI is a software interface defined by the firm Microsoft for Windows for the use of multimedia hardware components (eg sound cards).

Megabyte

A unit of measurement abbreviated as Mb, that corresponds to 2^{20} bytes (= 1,048,576 bytes). When hard disk sizes are given, they are often calculated using the value of 1,000,000 bytes.

MF-2

Abbreviation for Multi-function keyboard type 2. MF-2 denotes the current keyboard standard for PCs today, with 102 keys and three control lights.

MFM

Abbreviation for Modified Frequency Modulation. This procedure is nowadays used only for storing data on floppy disks. It also used to be important for hard disks.

MIDI

Abbreviation for Musical Instruments Digital Interface. The MIDI standard links electronic musical instruments with the computer.

MIPS

Abbreviation for Million Instructions Per Second. The unit of measure gives a starting point for the speed of the CPU.

Mirroring

In this procedure for data backup, the data are mirrored on a second disk. In the event of a hardware crash, the synchronous copy is still available on the second drive (see also **RAID**).

Modem

Abbreviation for Modulator/demodulator. A modem converts analog signals coming via the telephone line into digital information (and vice versa). It is used for data transfer. The transfer rate of modern modems can be up to 33,600 bps.

Motherboard

The main board in a computer. Besides the processor, this contains the **RAM** memory and the components required to run the other hardware, as well as the **BIOS**, **DMA** controller, **interrupt** controller, **cache** controller and various slots.

MPC

Abbreviation for Multimedia Personal Computer. This standard laid down by the computer industry specifies a minimum requirement of a multimedia computer.

The MPC level 2 of 1993, for example, specifies a processor of 486 SX and upwards with a HighColor graphics card, a 16-bit sound card, 8 Mb RAM and a double-speed CD-ROM drive.

MPEG

Abbreviation for Motion Pictures Expert Group. In considering video, this group of experts has developed a very efficient standard for compressing the picture and the sound. As for PCs, there are special expansion cards that can use the so-called MPEG-2 process for reproducing and compressing videos.

MPR

Abbreviation for the Swedish Council for Measuring and Testing Equipment (Swedish standard).

MTBF

Abbreviation for Mean Time Between Failures. It describes the average operating period for technical devices until a defect occurs. A CD-ROM drive, for example, has an MTBF of 10,000 hours.

Multi-frequency monitor

A monitor which can be automatically set to different frequencies and screen resolutions, as opposed to the fixed-frequency monitor.

Multi-I/O card

A plug-in card which simultaneously contains an IDE controller for hard disks and floppy disk drives, as well as further I/O interfaces (serial and parallel ports).

Multi-scan monitor

Another name for the multi-frequency monitor.

Multi-session capable

If a writable CD-ROM (particularly a **Photo CD**) is still not full after the first session, the opportunity exists to fill the CD-ROM up in further sessions. Every session is closed with a special feature. With older, single-session capable drives, this closing feature can sometimes be misinterpreted as the end of the CD-ROM.

Multisync

A trade mark name introduced by the firm NEC for a multi-frequency monitor. As NEC was one of the first manufacturers to bring out such monitors, the name is still used synonymously today.

297

N

Natural keyboard

A particularly ergonomic keyboard developed by Microsoft. It is split in the middle, and the two halves are positioned at a slightly inclined angle to each other. Since then, there have been many budget imitations of the relatively expensive original.

Null modem cable

The null modem cable provides a simple means of connecting two PCs together via their serial ports. This cable does not simply join all leads together, but the sending and receiving leads must be swapped within the cable. In this way, a simple data transfer is possible at low speeds of up to 115 bps.

O

OCR

Abbreviation for Optical Character Recognition. With the help of this procedure, the letters from a page of text scanned in as a graphics file can be recognised and then converted into a text file.

OEM version

Abbreviation for Original Equipment Manufacturer version. An OEM manufacturer uses software and hardware components of other manufacturers and markets them as his own devices. With software, the problem often is that the software manufacturer offers no support or upgrade services with OEM versions. Often the OEM supplier has to draw up his own handbooks. This is why such software is correspondingly cheaper.

OLE

Abbreviation for Object Linking and Embedding. The OLE procedure was developed by Microsoft to facilitate the exchange of data between various Windows applications. OLE is an expansion of the DDE interface. The special feature here is that the data entered into other applications remains firmly linked to its original application.

On-board

Components which, instead of being a plug-in card, are already integrated into the **motherboard**, are called on-board. With modern boards, the hard disk controller and the interface controller, for example, are already accommodated on the board. One advantage here is that the components can be manufactured more cheaply, and are better suited to the motherboard. However, the disadvantage is usually poorer upgradeability to take advantage of new developments.

OPL

The OPL chip is manufactured by the firm Yamaha, and is commonly used on sound cards for sound creation. Recently, the OPL-3 version has gained acceptance as a standard for SoundBlaster cards. The OPL chip was first used by the firm Adlib on sound cards. The current OPL-4 chip does not provide synthetically created sounds any more, but can fall back on a library of digitalised sounds.

OS

Abbreviation for the Operating System of a computer (eg MS-DOS, Windows or OS/2).

OSD

Abbreviation for On-Screen Display. With modern monitors, screen options are usually selected from a menu displayed on screen.

299

Overdrive

The overdrive processors by Intel represent easily manageable upgrade technology. On motherboards that are equipped with this upgradeability, the overdrive processor is either inserted into its own **ZIF socket** or is simply exchanged for the old processor. Increases in performance of between 40% and 200% can thus be obtained. Overdrive technology has been available from Intel since the 486 generation.

P

Paging

A procedure for organising memory into pages. These are then further divided into lines and columns. With writing and reading access to the same line on a page, only the column address is transmitted. This procedure naturally leads to enormously faster access (up to 20%).

Parallel port

The parallel port (or LPT port) is a connection for external devices, such as the printer, to the computer. Here the data is sent parallel, ie bytewise, in both directions. The speed is correspondingly higher than with serial transmission.

Parity

The sum of the digits in a byte, which is called parity, can either equal zero or one. It is used for error checking in storage or data transfer.

Parity

A parity check in memory modules is often described as parity. Bit errors in the memory components in the chip set can usually be detected in this way. In the event of an error, the computer then breaks off its work and reports Parity error. Thanks to the really reliable **DRAM** technology, the recent trend has been to use modules with no parity, as they are very much cheaper.

Partition

A hard disk can be divided into logical areas, so that these individual partitions can be addressed by the operating system as different logical drives. The first (primary) partition usually denotes the boot partition. When the computer is started up, it is from here that the operating system is loaded.

PCI bus

The PCI bus is a local bus system further developed by the firm Intel. It is designed as a more efficient alternative to the **VESA local bus** system, and has quickly gained acceptance as a standard, especially as the older VESA technology is being pushed to its limits in modern Pentium systems. The PCI standard exists in the current 2.0 version (version 2.1 is in preparation), and is mainly used by expansion cards such as hard disk controllers or video cards. With the corresponding **BIOS**, PCI provides a **plug & play** function for the automatic installation of plug-in cards. The maximum data throughput rate is given as 132 Mb/sec for PCs.

PCL

Abbreviation for Printer Control Language. PCL is a page description language developed by the firm Hewlett Packard. In the current PCL-5 version, this language also contains the **HPGL** standard for vector graphics. Most laser printers nowadays work in accordance with the PCL-5 standard at least. In the semi-professional field, it is preferred to the similar **PostScript** for reasons of cost.

301

PCMCIA

Abbreviation for Personal Computer Memory Card International Association. The PCMCIA identifies a standard for plug-in cards in cheque card format. More than 300 firms in the hardware and software field have agreed to this PC card architecture, providing network adapters, modems, hard disks and RAM memory as plug-in cards.

Pentium Pro

The successor to the Pentium processor by the firm Intel is called the Pentium Pro. The most striking difference from its predecessor is the integration of the second-level cache in the processor housing. Further acceleration was achieved with a new processing technique. Initial analysis and optimisation take place even before the commands are executed. The improvements in performance, however, can only be fully exploited with a 32-bit system. Old 16-bit programs run only at roughly the same speed or even more slowly than with a normal Pentium processor.

Performance

The performance denotes the efficiency and speed of a PC system or of individual components.

PGA

Abbreviation for Pin Grid Array. The PGA is a design in which Intel, for example, manufactures its processors today. It consists of a ceramic housing from which 168 to 273 slightly flexible contact pins project downwards. These processors are plugged into one socket (cf **PQFP**).

Photo CD

A procedure specially developed by the firm Kodak to store photographs digitally. Normal negative films are thus digitalised and burned into a CD for the customer. Approximately 50 pictures in three different resolutions will fit onto a CD. With a special playback unit, the pictures can be viewed on any television set. At the same time, however, they can also be read by any standard CD-ROM drive.

Pipeline burst cache

The burst mode is used in conjunction with the second-level cache. In this mode, the data can be transferred more quickly, as the whole memory address is not given. Only the beginning of the address and the number of data elements are given here. In addition, with pipeline burst cache, several such burst accesses can also be started at the same time.

Pipelining

A technique used in processor design whereby the elements involved in processing the commands are scheduled repeatedly and can work simultaneously.

Pixel

Abbreviation of the words 'picture element'. A pixel is the smallest display unit of a picture (a dot).

Plug & play

This system is designed to simplify the installation of expansion cards, just like the slogan 'plug in and get started'. In particular, this means doing without jumpers or complicated BIOS installations, because the plug & play (P&P) system takes care of that automatically. The only prerequisite for it is a suitable BIOS, as well as P&P adapter cards.

P&P

Abbreviation for Plug & Play.

POST

Abbreviation for Power-On Self-Test. POST denotes the self-test which the computer (the BIOS) carries out after being switched on. The signals (mainly sound signals) that indicate the result of this test are called POST codes.

303

PostScript

A special page description language which was mainly developed for the output of data on the printer. Contrary to common practice elsewhere, the pages are not issued dot for dot, but by means of specific instructions (eg a circle instead of X and Y). Nowadays, PostScript printers are principally used in the professional field for high-quality output.

Power supply

The electricity supply (mains unit).

PQFP

Abbreviation for Plastic Quad Flat Pack. PQFP denotes a design in which Intel, for example, manufactures its processors today. It consists of a plastic housing, and is fitted on the outside with 196 spring contacts (cf **PGA**).

PRN

The **LPT** 1 standard printer port is often described as PRN (printer), eg in the MS-DOS operating system.

PROM

Abbreviation for Programmable Read-Only Memory. Programmed information can be permanently stored and retrieved again and again from these memory components. The data are permanently written into the chip with an EPROM burner. Such PROMs are used, for example, for the BIOS of a PC. Further developments are **EPROMs** and **EEPROMs**.

Processor upgrade

Many motherboards are so equipped that the **CPU** can be exchanged later for a more efficient processor. Usually this procedure takes almost no time at all, and considerably enhances performance.

Protected mode

From the 286 processor up to today's Pentium, the RAM can be managed in protected mode as well as in real mode. The data of the various programs in the memory are protected here from mutual access. The maximum amount of manageable memory depends on the width of the address bus. For the 386 processor and upwards, it amounts to 32 bits, which corresponds to 4 Gb of memory.

Processor clone

The processors made by the firm Intel, which have gained worldwide acceptance as a standard for computer CPUs, are constantly being copied by other firms. As a result, the compatibility of 486 processors is often very high, as is their performance, and they sometimes cost much less than the originals. However, there are no really competitive Pentium clones so far.

PS/2 mouse

Many Pentium motherboards provide their own mouse port. The advantage of this is that no valuable serial ports are used up. However, the disadvantage is that a special outlet is involved and an expensive PS/2 mouse or suitable adapter is required.

PS/2 module

In the early 1990s, PS/2 modules were only used in the PS/2 series of computers by IBM. In recent years, however, their advantages for other systems were also recognised, with the result that these memory components have developed into a standard. PS/2 modules are fitted with a total of 72 contacts on the underside, and are thus easy to identify. Such modules are available in sizes of up to 64 Mb.

Q

QuadSpeed

Expensive CD-ROM drives with QuadSpeed quadruple speed reach data transfer rates of about 600 Kb/sec, sextuple drives about 900 Kb/sec, and octuple drives about 1200 Kb/sec.

QIC

Abbreviation for Quarter-Inch Cartridge. The QIC standard mainly denotes the design of a magnetic tape cassette which is used in streamer drives for data backup. Cassette memory capacities range from 40 Mb up to 2 Gb.

R

Radial stepper motor

A motor that works with extreme precision and is used in hard disks to move the writing and reading heads from track to track.

RAID

Abbreviation for Redundant Array of Inexpensive Disks. The RAID is technology for data backup. At level 1 of the RAID backup stage, a hard disk is simply mirrored on a second disk in a mirroring or **duplexing** procedure. If parts of the first disk crash, a second copy is still available on the second hard disk. With the RAID level 5 procedure, usually five hard disks are operated by a common controller. Test totals of the individual sectors are divided evenly between the disks. If one disk fails, usually all of the data can be reconstructed by means of the other drives, and the system can resume work without any interruption.

RAM

Abbreviation for Random Access Memory; a memory component which can be written and read with free access. It is used as a normal memory store in every PC. There are other types of RAM such as **DRAM**, **SRAM**, **SDRAM** and EDO-RAM.

RAM-DAC

Abbreviation for Random-Access Memory – Digital-to-Analogue Converter. This element converts the digital colour data of a graphics card into analogue signals for output to the monitor.

Read-Only Memory

In a read-only memory, data can be stored once and then has to be called up every time. It requires no constant voltage to store the information. It is usually referred to by the acronym ROM.

Real mode

With PC processors of the first generation (Intel 8086s and 8088s), real mode was the only one with which the operating system could address the memory. In this mode, program code and data are located in an area of memory, and cannot be protected from each other. Each program thus has unrestricted access to the whole area. Memory positions are addressed with the physical address, and storage requirements are relayed via the address bus without being checked. In real mode, a maximum storage area of 1 Mb can be addressed. The next generation of processors should also have a protected mode.

Refresh

Unlike S**RAMs**, **DRAM** memory components have to be provided with refresh voltage at regular intervals, so that its information is not lost.

307

Refresh rate

The screen refresh rate indicates the number of pictures per second produced. At lower values, the picture flickers and the human eye reacts irritably. Monitors with values of more than 72 Hz are considered to be ergonomically sensible.

Register

The various areas of memory in which addresses, operands, parameters and interim results are stored are described as the register.

Resident

Programs which remain permanently in the background of the RAM are described as memory-resident. They are used as hardware drivers, for example.

RET

Abbreviation for Resolution Enhancement Technology. This procedure developed by the firm Hewlett Packard is designed to increase the quality of the printout from a laser printer. It is a special procedure to smooth out the edges (of the so-called step effect). Because the resolution is constant, the beholder is given the impression of higher resolution. This technique is now being offered by various manufacturers, under different names, of course.

RISC processor

Abbreviation for Reduced Instruction Set Computer. With its simplified and reduced set of commands, this processor facilitates the considerably faster execution of individual commands. More complex commands, however, must be carried out by a series of machine codes.

ROM

Abbreviation for Read-Only Memory, ie memory from which already stored information can always be read, over and over again. A ROM memory is used in the BIOS, for example.

RS 232 interface

The RS 232 interface is the most widely used standard for the serial port. Most computers nowadays are fitted with such a 9-pin or 24-pin socket. Devices such as the mouse or the modem can be plugged in here.

RTC

Abbreviation for Real-Time Clock. The RTC is the device on the motherboard which looks after the correct date and time of day.

S

Sampling

In digital processing, sampling denotes the digitalisation or scanning of an original picture or sound.

Video data can be sampled with a scanner or a video camera, and audio data are usually sampled with a sound card.

Screen savers

These programs, running in the background, are meant to darken the screen or display, constantly changing screen contents, in the event of any inactivity. With earlier screens, the burning-in of blank screen structures into the phosphor layer was a real problem. With modern colour monitors and graphic user surfaces, there is no longer any real need for a screen saver. However, humorous screen savers for entertainment or advertising purposes are enjoying a real boom.

SCSI

Abbreviation for Small Computer System Interface. The SCSI standard allows the operation of up to seven peripheral devices with one controller. At the same time, the installation of several SCSI controllers in one PC is no problem. Besides hard disks, other devices such as scanners can also be connected. The devices are then connected to a single cable, one behind the other. The last device is fitted with a terminator, thus identifying the end of the bus.

SCSI-2

The current SCSI-2 standard which, in contrast to the SCSI-1 standard, consistently aims for synchronous data transfer, facilitating transfer rates of up to 10 Mb/sec. SCSI-1 facilitates data transfer of up to 3.3 Mb/sec in normal asynchronous working mode, and rates of up to 5 Mb/sec in faster synchronous modes. (An expansion option for the SCSI-2 standard is Wide SCSI).

SCSI-3

This standard, also known as the Ultra SCSI standard, is still not completely specified. It is designed to facilitate data transfer rates of up to 100 Mb/sec. However, in view of the still very expensive 110-pin cable, it is still meaningless in practice.

S-DRAM

Abbreviation for Synchronous DRAM. A further development of the **DRAM**. These modules offer marginal speed advantages.

Sectors

Hard disks consist of several magnetically coated disks arranged one above the other. Each individual disk is divided into tracks which run in circles round the central axis, and the tracks are divided into sectors.

Semiconductor

In modern semiconductor technology, memory components are manufactured which are characterised by faster access times and constantly shrinking dimensions (cf **RAM** and **ROM** storage).

Serial port

The serial port (or COM port) is a connection to the computer for external devices such as the mouse or the modem. Data are sent serially, ie bit by bit, in both directions.

Shadow RAM

Most BIOS types provide a so-called shadow RAM function. It is used for copying parts of the slower ROM system into the faster RAM memory. As more and more operating systems nowadays directly address the hardware by by-passing the BIOS system, this function will be come more and more meaningless.

SIMM

Abbreviation for Single In-line Memory Module. These storage modules have 30 contacts on the underside. They mainly consist of eight components or nine components (with **parity**). The maximum size of a SIMM is 4 Mb. Latterly, SIMMs have been largely superseded by **PS/2 modules**.

SIMM shuttle

The SIMM-PS/2 adapter, known as the SIMM shuttle, makes it possible to still use old SIMM memory modules in boards fitted with PS/2 connections. For this purpose, four or eight SIMM modules are plugged into one adapter. This 72-pin adapter can now be used as a **PS/2 module**. With the continuing drop in the prices of PS/2 modules, however, this adapter is hardly of any importance any more, and using it can pose many technical problems.

Single-session

In contrast to the multi-session capable CD-ROM drives which are in common use nowadays, old drives can often read only the first session completed on a **photo CD**.

SIO

Abbreviation for Serial Input/Output. This chip acts as the controller for serial data transfer. A **UART** circuit is usually used in PCs.

SIP

Abbreviation for Single In-line Package (cf **DIP**).

Slot

The plug-in connections on the motherboard which can accommodate the expansion cards are called slots.

Slow refresh

DRAM components of a PC are normally refreshed at intervals of 15 microseconds. In some BIOS installations, this clock rate can be extended to roughly every 60 microseconds.

SLSI

Abbreviation for Super Large-Scale Integration. SLSI denotes a degree of integration for a chip. At this level 100,000 transistor functions can be accommodated in one chip.

SPOOL

Abbreviation for Simultaneous Peripheral Operations On Line. The spooler is a special program which manages printing jobs waiting in a queue and stores them temporarily. They are gradually completed by the printer, while the user can immediately deal with the next job.

SRAM

Abbreviation for Static RAM memory. SRAM is a **RAM** memory component which, in contrast to **DRAM**, holds the information even without any constant cyclical refreshment. They are used at access speeds of 15 – 30 nanoseconds, as cache memory, for example.

SSI

Abbreviation for Statens Stralskydds Institut (Swedish Institute of Protection against Radiation), which was the first to publish guidelines on low-radiation monitors. Since then, these guidelines have been superseded, first by MPR-II and later by TCO-92.

Stepper motor

A motor which works with extreme precision, used in hard disks, for example, to move the writing and reading heads from track to track.

Swap file

A swap file deals with a file which has been taken out of storage. If the **RAM** memory actually available is no longer sufficient, parts of the RAM are temporarily taken out of storage on the hard disk. This technique is used by Windows, for example. Advantage: Larger applications can run even on smaller hardware platforms. Disadvantage: The hard disk naturally works far more slowly than real RAM memory.

Swedish standard

Jargon for the standard laid down by the Swedish Council for Measuring and Testing Equipment (MPR for short), which specifies the limits of radiation emitted by monitors. This standard was drawn up in collaboration with the Swedish Employees' Trade Union (TCO). Modern low-radiation monitors nowadays comply at least with the revised MPR II standard.

Synchronous

In synchronous data transfer, both transmitter and receiver are synchronised. The receiver sends confirmation at the same time as the data is received, while the transmitter is already sending the next lot of data (as opposed to **asynchronous** data transfer).

Synchronous cache

Another name for burst cache. See **pipeline burst cache**.

T

TCO

Abbreviation for the Swedish Employees' Trade Union. Its collaboration resulted in tighter forms of radiation limits for computer monitors. Testing in accordance with the TCO-92 standard sets much lower limits than the MPR-II.

Termination

Both of the two physical ends of an **SCSI** bus must be closed with a terminator. This termination has become necessary because of possible long cable lengths. Without terminators, any interference would be reflected at the end of the cable and cause further interference.

Topless SIMM

SIMM modules in which the silicon wafers are directly wired to the board are called topless SIMMs. They can be recognised by the fact that small, black blobs of resin are placed on top instead of the chip housing. These modules are also called COB (Chip On Board) SIMMs.

Touch pad

Small, touch-sensitive surface which reacts to finger movements. The touch pad replaces the mouse or trackball in notebooks.

TPI

Abbreviation for Tracks Per Inch. The number of tracks per inch on a hard disk is given in TPIs. It is an indication of the amount of data to be stored.

Trackball

The trackball is a kind of inverted mouse. A ball is moved directly with the fingers, with the normal mouse buttons placed in front. The advantage of this input device is that it requires less space and no smooth mat underneath.

Tracks

Hard disks consist of several magnetically coated disks arranged one above the other. Each individual disk is divided into tracks which run in circles round the central axis and are divided into sectors.

Troubleshooting

The search for the causes of and cures for hardware or software faults is called troubleshooting.

True Colour

True Colour is jargon for a depth of colour that roughly corresponds with human colour perception. So the term could be paraphrased as 'true-to-life colours' (or even 'genuine colour display'). The True Colour palette of colours contains 16.7 million colours, which indicates a 24-bit depth of colour (cf **High Colour**).

Turbo LED

This lamp diode indicates whether the PC is in turbo mode.

TWAIN

Abbreviation for Transmit Windows Advanced Interface. This standard interface makes it possible for scanners made by different manufacturers to be used in various Windows programs. Any TWAIN-compatible scanner can be used in any TWAIN-compatible application. In practice, however, problems are often caused as a result of not completely consistent interpretation of the standard.

Typematic rate

In **CMOS**, there is usually an opportunity to set the key repetition rate precisely. This option is then used whenever a key is kept pressed down for a longer time.

U

UART

Abbreviation for Universal Asynchronous Receiver/Transmitter. The UART component is the essential element in a serial port. Types such as the NS 8250 or 16450 are normally used in PCs. In fact, the type 16550 has been exclusively used recently. With its built-in FIFO memory, it enhances transmission security in multitasking environments.

ULSI

Abbreviation for Ultra Large-Scale Integration. ULSI denotes a degree of integration for a chip. At this level, from one million to 100 million transistor functions can be accommodated in one chip.

UPS

Abbreviation for Uninterrupted Power Supply. Connecting a UPS to a computer is becoming extremely simple. It is merely inserted between the mains plug and the socket. First of all, it filters out the voltage fluctuations which occur in any mains supply on a daily basis. In addition, in the event of a power failure, it provides sufficient energy over a certain period at least to save the data and run the system down properly.

V

VESA

Abbreviation for Video Electronics Standard Association, which has created various standards in the graphics area.

VESA local bus

Also known as the VL bus, this standard denotes an improved bus system which accelerates communication between the CPU and peripherals. The system, which now exists in its current version 2.0, is used mainly for graphics cards and hard disk controllers. In contrast to the conventional **ISA bus**, better speed is achieved with an increased bus speed of up to 40 MHz (instead of 8.3 MHz) and a data width of 32 bits (instead of 16 bits).

VFAT

Abbreviation for Virtual File Allocation Table (cf **FAT**). VFAT is an expansion of the FAT system which is used in Windows for Workgroups 3.11 and in Windows 95, for example. Besides the speed advantage of its 32-bit access, file names with a length of up to 255 characters are now possible under Windows 95.

Video CD

According to the standard adopted in 1993, a video CD contains up to 74 minutes of video and audio data which have been recorded by the **MPEG** process.

VLB

Abbreviation for VESA local bus.

317

VLSI

Abbreviation for Very Large-Scale Integration. VLSI is the name given to a chip integration level. At this level, 10,000 to 1,000,000 transistor functions can be accommodated on one chip.

VRAM

Abbreviation for Video RAM. VRAM components are **DRAM** storage areas which have been developed principally for graphics cards and have separate input and output ports.

W

Wait states

An excessively fast processor with peripherals working at correspondingly lower speeds must insert one or more waiting states in order to ensure correct data transfer.

Whetstone

A benchmark test which principally measures the calculating performance of the arithmetical co-processor. Nowadays, it is really only of historical importance.

Wide SCSI

Expansion option of the SCSI-2 standard. Data can be moved here with a 16-bit or 32-bit wide bus. This results in a multiplication of the maximum transfer rates of up to 40 Mb. In addition, the number of devices which can be operated on one bus is increased to 16 or 32.

WORM

Abbreviation for Write Once Read Multiple. A WORM disk is a storage medium which can be written once with a special drive, and can then be read again in any CD-ROM drive.

WRAM

Abbreviation for Windows RAM. Just like **VRAM** components, the newer WRAM storage areas are chips specially designed for video cards. In addition, they possess some functions implemented for faster output of graphical pixels. The data throughput rate has been increased by about 50% compared to VRAMs.

WYSIWYG

Abbreviation for What You See Is What You Get. This means that whatever appears on the screen in an application can be printed out in the same form. This saves test prints and makes it possible to judge the appearance of a printout while it is still on screen.

Z

ZIF socket

Abbreviation for Zero Insertion Force Socket. Modern Pentium motherboards are normally fitted with a ZIF socket into which the processor is plugged. To enable the processor to be used, the lever moved to one side is merely released and pushed upwards.

ZIP drive

Newly developed alternative disk system which can be compared to a disk drive. The storage media have a capacity of 100 Mb (cf **JAZ** drive).

Zone bit recording

Recording process which takes into account the different geometry of the tracks on magnetic disks. Given the same disk size, this can result in a capacity which is increased by as much as 40%.

327